You Can Start a Website

You Can Start a Website

Step-by-Step Strategy and Directions to Design and
Market Your Own WordPress Website or Blog

Jane Moyer

Published by New Century Leadership LLC, P.O. Box 223, Hinsdale IL 60522

Library of Congress Control Number: 2013920764

ISBN: 978-1-940975-01-6

Contents

Start Your Own Website
Affordable. Flexible. Yours.

Do you want to be able to:
- *Share your message, service or product with the world?*
- *Create an affordable, flexible website or blog yourself?*
- *Learn an important 21st century communication skill?*

In this book, I'll show you how you can create your own website or blog, even if you have little or no technical experience. *If I can, you can.*

This book is for people who have ideas, content, services or products, but perhaps not a lot of technical knowledge or a large budget. Many smart, creative people with good ideas get bogged down when faced with the task of launching a website. They often feel overwhelmed with choices, confused by technical terms, and worn down by the number and variety of tasks involved. They may get boxed in by making decisions in the wrong order. If they can afford to hire help, they sometimes find that the web designer is quirky or doesn't "get" them. If they do get their site launched, they often find that, by itself, it achieves little.

If any of that sounds like you, take heart. The aim of this book is to simplify the process and help you set yourself up to achieve the outcomes you want. While launching a website does require time, thought and energy, I hope to save you some of each of those and make the process both more enjoyable and more successful for you.

The steps we'll be covering to create your website are these:
1. *Get Prepared: Strategy and Planning*
2. *Choose Your Website Tools*
3. *Set Up Your Site*
4. *Develop Effective Content*
5. *Market to Build Traffic*
6. *Get Results*
7. *Protect and Maintain Your Site*

This book will take you through not just the practical details involved in launching your site, but also the strategic thinking that will lead to your desired results. Since putting up your website is only part of a successful internet strategy, it will also touch on related processes and resources often needed in combination with your website to obtain optimal results.

Reading the book will be helpful, I hope, but moving forward by taking action to successfully launch your website is most important. You'll find a series of worksheets throughout the book designed to help you with each step along the way. Use them to develop your strategy, experiment with content and design, organize processes and record important information and decisions.

There are many pieces to put together, so be patient with yourself. It's all within your reach. *If I can, you can.* Let's go.

My Story: How I Set Up a WordPress Website Myself
If I can, you can.

I wanted to be able to set up and experiment with some websites without having to pay a web developer $1,000–$2,500 or more for each one. I was what you might call "techno-challenged", though. I knew little about graphics, I freak out when my computer freezes up, and I know no html code.

In 2005, I paid a web developer $2,000 to set up a business website for me. She did a beautiful job. While I still love my web developer, as my business grew and changed I tired of having to contact her and pay $50–75 every time I wanted to make a small copy change.

I thought I had solved the problem, at least somewhat, by using Apple's iWeb software, but they discontinued it in 2012. Other software I looked at seemed expensive, daunting and difficult to learn. Free "easy" software promoted by web hosts turned out to be very limited when I actually installed it. (Note: If you truly only need something very simple (ex. 1–5 pages, basic format, no blogging, few features), I'll share some suggestions in the "Website Software" section.)

I explored several products and services and made many mistakes and false-starts in search of a solution. I spent early mornings and late nights researching and experimenting.

An Easier Way
Now, let me make it easier for you.

The primary resource that now makes it possible for regular folks to create websites is WordPress, a free content software. But it does require some learning and there are still many other issues to sort through. It took me several months, much research and experimentation and a great deal of perseverance to create my first site. I've created several now and, using the information and system I'll cover in this book, I can now set one up (not including writing the content, artistic fiddling and setting up other related systems) in a couple of hours.

In case you're curious, here's a link for the first website I created, so you can see what is possible for a total beginner: www.musicbeginnersguide.com.

Soon a variety of friends and clients — authors, musicians, entrepreneurs, coaches, consultants, small business owners, and moms — began asking me for a little help when they wanted to start a website or blog. It was thrilling to see what these interesting, smart, but non-technical people could build when they had a few good creative tools and a little guidance on resources so they didn't get bogged down trying to figure out too many details in the process.

About This Book
In this book, I'll be outlining the website creation process, sharing tips and recommending some resources based on my experience. My aim is to use my research and experience to save you a lot of time and effort.

A few important notes and disclaimers: Things change constantly in this internet world — I plan to update information in revised editions as I am aware of changes, but can't guarantee perfect accuracy at any time.

This is an information resource intended to help with the basics of setting up a site. You may need to supplement this with additional professional help on specific tasks and issues. Every situation is different, so while I will give some tips and general suggestions, you will need to make your own choices about what is best for you and your own site.

While you can spend more if you want or need extra features and services, the basics of your own website will likely cost $60–120 per year. (Many web hosting companies offer special rates the first year and then raise them as time goes on, so check that out when you sign up.)

Regarding the products highlighted here, I've included the ones I've chosen myself after much research and sometimes additional options that present either different features or a good alternative. For your convenience, in the "Resources Mentioned" section near the back of the book, website addresses (current at the time of writing, but subject to change) are given for resources mentioned throughout the book. (In the ebook version, links have been included throughout to take you directly to resource providers' sites.) While my aim is to make this convenient and save you time, I cannot, of course, guarantee any third party resources, so please examine these in light of your own needs and their current capabilities.

Congratulations on your decision to create your own website. Get ready to play with it. Be patient with yourself. It may take some experimentation, but, if you persist, you'll get the hang of it! Enjoy the process and the feeling of satisfaction you will get when your own site comes to life!

First Steps

Checklist: First Steps

Start by laying a strong foundation for your project. In this section, we'll cover the following initial steps:

Define Your Goals

- ☐ Purpose
- ☐ Outcomes
- ☐ Type of Site
- ☐ Visitors

Sketch Out Your Design

- ☐ Research Sites With a Similar Purpose and Audience for Ideas
- ☐ Sketch Out Your Layout
- ☐ Make a Rough Sketch of Your Navigation

Get Ready Mentally and Practically

- ☐ Adopt an Internet Mindset
- ☐ Start to Record Key Information
- ☐ Prepare to Budget
- ☐ Set a Timeline

Identify Your Website Purpose

Before you do anything else, get clear on the purpose of your website and the audience you aim to attract.

Your Purpose:
- *What is the overall purpose of your website?*
- *What results do you want to achieve with it?*
- *How does a website fit with your greater purpose or business?*

Your Audience:
- *Who do you want to attract to your website?*
- *What would they be looking for?*
- *What words would they use to describe themselves and what they are looking for?*
- *What will they do as a result of visiting your site?*

Invest some time and thought upfront to answering these questions. Then keep your answers top of mind while choosing your tools, setting up your site, developing your content and coordinating your website efforts with your greater purpose.

Begin with the exercises that follow which are designed to spur your thinking and help you move forward strategically.

Website Strategy: Purpose

Get clear first on the purpose of your website.

Here are some purposes a website can fulfill. What is important to you?

I want my website to be ...

- ☐ Fun

- ☐ An outlet for my ideas

- ☐ A brochure for my business, products or services

- ☐ A vehicle for building a mailing list

- ☐ A means of generating revenue

- ☐ An online store

- ☐ An information resource

- ☐ A community for exchange or ideas and information

- ☐

- ☐

- ☐

- ☐

You might have multiple reasons for having a website. If so, prioritize them here.

My top reasons for having a website are:

1.

2.

3.

Website Strategy: Outcomes

What would you like to happen as a result of someone visiting your website?

Ideally, my visitors will ...

- ☐ Smile
- ☐ Come back for another visit
- ☐ Feel inspired
- ☐ Feel informed
- ☐ Support a cause
- ☐ Know me
- ☐ Like me
- ☐ Trust me
- ☐ Call me
- ☐ Request more information
- ☐ Download a report
- ☐ Join my mailing list
- ☐ Visit my location
- ☐ Comment
- ☐ Become a community member
- ☐ Solve a problem
- ☐ Make a decision
- ☐ Refer to me via social media — "like" me, tweet about me, post me, blog about me
- ☐ Click on an ad
- ☐ Send a donation
- ☐ Hire me
- ☐ Purchase my product or service
- ☐ Purchase someone else's product or service
- ☐ Register for an event
- ☐ Take action

If you identified multiple results, take a moment to prioritize them. What is most important?

Keep these outcomes in mind as you design your website.

Types of Websites: The Money Question

Before you design your website, one important factor to determine is the role money-making might play. Which best fits your intention:

☐ *I don't care about making money with my website. I'm creating it for personal reasons, for fun, for others to enjoy or become better informed.*

☐ *While I don't plan to make money directly from my website, I hope to build relationships, interest and/or a reputation so others might engage with me, purchase from me, or hire me in the future.*

☐ *I'm not selling anything directly myself. I hope to make money through advertising and/or sales of other people's products.*

☐ *My purpose is to make money directly. I want visitors to purchase something from me via my website.*

☐ *Combination of the above. My priority is _____.*

Your answer will determine the type of site you need — Non-Commercial, Informational, or Commercial. Let's look at each type more closely:

Non-Commercial
For the Sake of It

☐ I don't care about making money with my website. I'm creating it for personal reasons, social reasons, for fun, for others to enjoy or become better informed.

Informational
Building Interest, Relationships and a Brand

☐ While I don't plan to make money directly from my website, I hope to build relationships, interest and/or a reputation so others might engage with me, purchase from me, or hire me in the future.

This type of site usually works hand-in-hand with other marketing and sales tools. It provides background information and other resources that might be of interest to a potential customer. Types of information sites include:

The Big Business Card: In this era, most businesses and organizations provide at least some basic information via a website. The website might include a description of products, services or events, biographical information, contact information, and information regarding hours and locations. This type of site doesn't drive business per se, but works in combination with other forms of information or marketing.

Portfolio or Brochure: This type of site showcases your work or products to build interest. It provides a convenient way for potential customers to get to know you and your work. For instance, an artist or photographer might showcase pieces or photos. An ad agency or graphic design business might post creative samples. A consultant might provide case studies or testimonials. A job seeker might provide a resume and portfolio of work samples.

Relationship Builder: This type of site encourages a potential customer to engage with you in order to build trust and interest. The site might provide information, tips, free reports and a community of people with similar interests.

Brand Builder: All of these types of informational sites can also help an individual or organization build their brand. The approach, language and graphics combine to give the visitor a "feel" for the individual or organization and what's unique about them. These sites can also combine with social media and other marketing tactics to build a reputation.

With this type of site, you will probably want to invite the visitor to take a small action step. For instance, sign up for a newsletter, join a community, request more information, schedule an appointment, download a report or coupon, "like" you on social media or "share" information.

Commercial: Indirect Sales
Advertising and Affiliate Marketing

☐ I'm not selling anything directly myself. I hope to make money through advertising and/or sales of other people's products.

With this type of site, you make money when a visitor clicks on ads (i.e. "pay per click" advertising) or makes a purchase as a result of clicking on an ad or link on your site (for example, through affiliate programs, commissions, referrals, or partner programs).

This type of site is usually some type of information resource — for instance it might provide news, reviews, a directory and other information.

In order to make money from this type of site, you must provide value to visitors and build traffic. Advertising and affiliate products must be relevant to your visitors and must be placed where they are most likely to engage.

To attract advertisers, you must provide content that is relevant and valuable. This type of site works best when it is targeted to an audience that is motivated and able to make a purchase.

Commercial: Direct Sales
Buy My Product or Service

☐ My purpose is to make money directly. I want visitors to purchase something from me via my website.

This type of site is set up to encourage the visitor to purchase your product or service. It will require a means of taking orders and payment, as well as a way to set up delivery of the product.

In addition to these practical arrangements, as you design your site, consider ways to increase sales. For instance, create trust by providing detailed information and authentic testimonials (Note: In internet commerce, the FTC requires these to represent *typical* results.) Eliminate risk for the customer by providing a money-back guarantee. Add an element of urgency by providing time-sensitive special offers. Create value by packaging together extra features and elements. Be sure that the ordering process is easy for the customer.

Types of Websites: The Blog Question

Another important decision to make before you design your website is whether it will be a blog (or include a blog).

What is a Blog?

A blog, short for "weblog", is a collection of "posts" or articles on a particular topic.

Blogs usually have a few common characteristics:
- **News:** New content is added on an ongoing basis.
- **Conversation:** Blogs give the feel of an online conversation. Visitors can usually leave comments. Blogs often present links to other related blogs (a "blogroll") and "feeds" that show the latest news from other sources of interest. Bloggers often read, quote, and link to other blogs.
- **Most Current Content Appears First**: Entries are usually organized in chronological order, with the most recent entry appearing on top. There is usually an archive of past articles. "Categories" and "Tags" are assigned to articles so that new visitors can easily find earlier content of interest.

Benefits of a Blog

A blog allows you to:
- Highlight new content
- Report news and react to current events
- Receive comments from readers
- Build a community
- Post content simultaneously on social media sites
- Show internet search engines you have added new content
- Keep top of mind with readers, potential customers and collaborators

To Blog or Not to Blog?

As you can see, blogging has many benefits. To be a successful blogger, though, you must continually come up with interesting content, build an audience and post regularly. It can be time-consuming and stressful, especially if you don't love to write. Moderating comments, writing responses and fighting off spam can also be time-consuming and stressful. Before you plunge in, ask yourself:
- Who will read your blog? There are now more than 250 million blogs online. What will make yours worth reading?
- Do you have sufficient content to post regularly?
- Do you have the time and inclination to post regularly?
- How will you manage comments?
- How will you avoid spam?

Blogging with Purpose

Bloggers have a variety of reasons for their work. Before you take the blogging plunge, get clear on your purpose and goals. How will you judge your success? Criteria bloggers use to gauge their success might include:

- Number of visitors
- Number of comments
- Page views, clicks, click-through rate
- Website-specific or business-specific results

Website Strategy: Visitors

Think about your potential website visitors:

- Who do you want to attract to your website?
- What would they be looking for?
- What will they do as a result of visiting your site?

Describe your ideal website visitor. Are they likely to be a certain gender, age, or type? Are they involved in a certain profession, with a particular hobby or cause? Do they share common interests? Are they likely to think or behave in certain ways?

They would describe themselves as ...

They are likely to have these desires:

They are likely to have these problems:

They would be looking for ... (information, ideas, solutions, products, services, results)

When searching for information, ideas, solutions, products, services or results, they might use these words:

As a result of visiting my site, they would:

Sketch Out Your Website Design

Next, sketch out a rough plan for your website. Don't use ink yet.

Before you design your site, take a look around the internet. Check out sites that have a similar purpose and audience — perhaps competitors' sites. If you plan to blog, search www.technorati.com or www.blogcatalog.com for blogs with related content.

Use the worksheet on the following page to note your observations.

Then, keeping your purpose and target audience in mind, consider ways to organize your site:

Home Page: What do you want your visitors to see first on the "Home" page? How will you make a good impression and then keep their interest?

Navigation: Make a chart of the pages you will have on your site and how they will be organized under "menus". How will you make it easy for visitors to find what they're looking for?

Header: A header is the area at the top of your website that stays constant. It typically includes a logo and a navigation menu. What major features need to be consistent?

Footer: A footer is the area at the bottom of your site that stays constant. It typically includes links to privacy policies, terms and conditions, and a copyright notice.

Sidebar: A sidebar is a column on either the right or left-hand side of the website page. It often includes items such as navigation, advertising, social media links, newsletter opt-in forms, blog categories or tags. What functions and features does your site need to incorporate?

Now, use the exercises that follow to make a rough sketch of your layout and navigation.

Website Design: Exploring the Internet

Explore the internet with an eye toward website design. Examine a variety of websites (and blogs, if you are planning to write a blog) noticing the "look", organization, features and design elements — color, fonts, layout and images — of each.

Look at sites or blogs in your own niche, but don't limit yourself to those. Notice what you like and don't like. Consider the results each site is aiming to achieve. Notice what works. Decide whether you'd want to return to that site and why. Gather ideas for your site.

Keep notes of your exploration here:

Website:

What's appealing:

What I don't like:

Ideas:

Website:

What's appealing:

What I don't like:

Ideas:

Website:

What's appealing:

What I don't like:

Ideas:

Website:

What's appealing:

What I don't like:

Ideas:

Website:

What's appealing:

What I don't like:

Ideas:

Website:

What's appealing:

What I don't like:

Ideas:

Website:

What's appealing:

What I don't like:

Ideas:

Website:

What's appealing:

What I don't like:

Ideas:

Website Design: Common Layouts

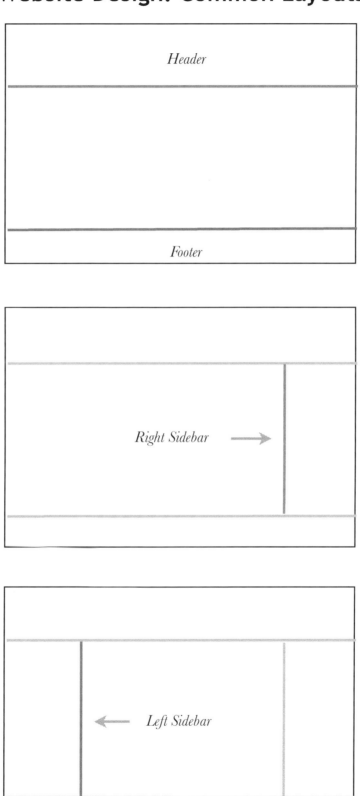

Now, sketch out potential layout choices for your website:

Website Design: Navigation

Navigation consists of the menus and links on your site that help the visitor find their way around. It directs them to the pages with the information they want.

Most website designs place the primary navigation at the top or going down the left side. Additional page labels might be found in sub-menus in the sidebars or in "drop-down" menus.

Some website design Themes allow for more than one menu. For instance, in addition to a Primary Menu at the top of the page, there might be a Footer Menu at the bottom. Additional features might also be placed in the sidebar or footer to help visitors find what they are looking for.

Navigation Principles

Good navigation is one of the most important factors in website success.

Make it Easy: As you design your navigation, keep in mind that its purpose is to help visitors find what they want. Look at it with "fresh eyes", as if you are a visitor coming there for the first time. Is the organization clear? Can you find what you want? Have a friend or two test this for you as well.

Use Standard Locations: Your visitors want to find things quickly. If they don't, they're likely to leave your site. They will be looking for your navigation at the top of the page, or, if it's not there, on the left side. Save your creativity for another time and put the menus where visitors expect them.

But Not Necessarily Standard Words: We have become accustomed to seeing standard navigation labels, such as "Home", "About", "Products", "Services", "Resources" and "Contact". While these may be appropriate, more specific words describing the pages, such as specific product categories or topics, work better for both humans and search engines.

Design for Search Engines, Too: Navigation is a key factor in search engine optimization. Use keywords potential visitors would be searching with in your menu labels.

Keep in mind that, while navigation "buttons" look cool, because they are images, the text is not visible to search engines, so text links may be a better choice.

Less is More Visible: Try to limit menu labels across the top to seven or fewer. That's about all the eye can take in and the brain can process at once.

Use Drop-down Menus Sparingly: They are more difficult for your visitor to use (and may also be more difficult for search engines to "crawl"). There's also a risk that your visitor will miss the top-level menu page completely. If you use drop-down menus, try to keep the number of drop-down items to a minimum — perhaps three or so.

Website Design: Sketch Out Your Navigation

Now, sketch out your website navigation.

Primary Menu

Your Primary Menu shows up consistently on each page and includes your major topics, as in the grey area below. Website templates often allow you to place additional sub-menu pages under these major topics. For examples, Primary Navigation might look like this:

Home	About	Topic 1	Topic 2	Topic 3	Topic 4	Contact
	Sub-topic	Sub-topic		Sub-topic		
		Sub-topic		Sub-topic		
		Sub-topic		Sub-topic		

Now, sketch out your website navigation.

Home						

If you'd like to try an alternative, sketch it here:

Home						

Sidebars

Most themes allow you to place additional content and features in the sidebar — usually on the right side. For blogs, typical sidebar choices include: Archives, a Calendar, Categories, Tags, a Blogroll, and a list of Recent Posts. Sidebars might also include customized Text, Images or Ads.

Sketch out some potential sidebars for your site here:

Sidebar

Sidebar

Footer

Next, think about what you'd like to have in the footer, the bottom area of the site that stays constant.

Elements often placed in the footer include: Privacy Policy, Terms & Conditions, Copyright, or Search. (If you are putting ads in the sidebar or using it for other purposes, you may put some of the other common sidebar elements in the footer.)

Privacy Policy	Terms & Conditions	Search
Copyright Notice		

Now, sketch out your footer:

Get Ready

Starting a website is a big and exciting project. You've laid a solid foundation by taking the time to define your goals well and plan your strategy. Here are two additional steps to take to set yourself up for internet success:

Prepare Mentally

The internet is an immense, quickly changing communications arena. Get ready to "think internet" as you work. The article that follows, "Adopt An Internet Mindset", will get you started.

Get Organized

As you work on your site, you'll need to take on big strategies and ideas, as well as many critical details. Set yourself up to keep track of it all.

- Start an information sheet to record all the key information about your site: Domain registrar, hosting company, usernames, passwords and any other important data you will need to keep organized and safe.
- Prepare to budget and keep track of your expenses. Plan for both your set-up and ongoing expenses.
- Devise a timeline and a plan to stay on track.

Use the three worksheets in this section throughout your website creation process to record your most critical information.

Adopt an Internet Mindset

It's a whole new world out there. To speed your progress and success, learn to "Think Internet". Here are ten tips to get you started:

It's a big world. It's a small world.
The internet opens up the whole world. The possibilities are endless.

Think BIG! You can communicate across the globe to more than 2.7 billion internet users.

Think small. Your messages will still be read by individuals one at a time. Make them personal and clear.

It changes quickly.
Breakthroughs and improvements in technology create constant change. Unless that's your only focus, it's hard to keep up completely. Think ahead as much as you can when you create your site so you're not quickly out-of-date. Choose tools that are likely to remain relevant and useful regardless of change. (For instance, I'm recommending WordPress, because, with more than 66 million users, I believe it will continue to evolve and incorporate improvements over time.) But don't sweat the details too much. You probably won't always need the latest and greatest.

We're all learning.
Because of constant change and improvements, we're always in learning mode. Be patient with yourself. As you learn and gain experience, each step will become easier. Resources such as this book and user forums can provide a good start. You'll learn a lot by just experimenting.

Write for three different "readers".
On the internet, you need to create your content keeping three different perspectives in mind. Write for 1) People, 2) Screens, and 3) Search Engines.

As with any other type of writing, you need to write for your human reader. Your writing needs to be clear and interesting. It needs to be well organized. Use "white space" to make it easy on the eye.

You also need to keep in mind how your content will look on the computer or other screen. (As more people are now viewing web content on tablets and mobile devices, for instance, I am recommending use of "responsive" themes that adjust content to the user's screen size.) Keep the most important content near the top of the page so the reader doesn't have to scroll down to view it. Be sure it loads quickly.

Lastly, if you want to be "found", you need to write for search engines, by incorporating "Keywords" that potential visitors would be using when searching for information.

Create value.

Information itself is of little value these days, because there is so much of it. The value is in what you do with it. How can you create value by synthesizing and interpreting information? How can you make it useful and interesting?

Target your content.

Who do you want to visit your site? What action do you want them to take? The more specifically you can define your audience, the easier it will be for them to find you. The clearer your purpose when you develop your content, the more likely you will accomplish your intended results. With more than 1 billion websites on the internet, you need to aim your content, descriptions and keywords as precisely as possible.

Give free stuff in order to get paid later.

Many services are free on the internet. For instance, you can set up a free email account. You can hold a free conference call and record it. You can create a free website. Many services have a free version, along with a paid version with additional features.

Likewise, many internet sites provide free information, reports and other goodies to build traffic and interest. Some do this to interest potential customers by giving them a taste of the benefits of a paid product or service, while others aim to make money from advertising placed on the site.

Build a list. Build a community.

Internet marketers have a saying: "The money is in the list". Start building a list right away, even if you don't have anything to sell right now. To send out mass emails legally, those on your list must have given their permission to receive email from you by "opting in" to your list.

If appropriate, develop your community further by incorporating social media tools into your site. For instance, add "share" buttons and incorporate plugins that will update your Facebook page and Twitter feeds automatically when you add to your blog.

Protect yourself.

Protect yourself from hackers by choosing a web host with good security and using strong passwords on your hosting and content sites. Protect your site from spam with anti-spam tools. Set up a system to back up your content regularly so you can restore it easily if needed.

You can't hide.

On the internet, it's a small world. There is an element of trust in dealing with people you will never see or meet in person. But nothing stays hidden for long. You develop a reputation online for the value you provide. Social media makes it possible to "spread the word", about either the good or bad, easily and quickly. Your reputation will follow you. So be aware and take care to do the right thing and build a reputation that will lead to long-term success.

Website Record

Website: www.

Domain Registration:
      Company:
      Username:
      Password:
      Renewal date:
      Auto-renew? *(If so, be sure a current credit card is on file with registrar.)*

Web Host:
      Company:
      Control Panel URL:
      Username:
      Password:
      Renewal date:
      Auto-renew? *(If so, be sure a current credit card is on file with web host.)*

Email Addresses:
      Address:
      Password:
      Forwarded to:

      Address:
      Password:
      Forwarded to:

WordPress Account:
      Log in at: www.(your url)/wp-admin
      Username:
      Password:

Google Account:
      Username:
      Password:

Other Important Account:
      Username:
      Password:

Other Important Account:
      Username:
      Password:

Website Budget

Year 1 Costs:

Webhosting (usually a discounted rate for new accounts):

Domain (if not included in webhosting plan):

Theme (if desired):

Other Services:

Total:

Year 2 Costs:

Webhosting:

Domain (if not included in webhosting plan):

Theme (if an annual fee):

Other Services:

Total:

Related Ongoing Expenses:

Website Timeline

Step	Target Date	Completed
Strategy: Identify Your Purpose, Define Outcomes, Determine Website Type, Describe Ideal Visitors		
Research: Gather Ideas		
Sketch Out Your Website Design		
Get Ready: Adopt an Internet Mindset. Start to Record Information, Prepare to Budget, Set a Timeline		
Choose Your Tools: Domains, Webhosting, Software		
Set Up Your Site: Install WordPress, Select a Theme, Adjust Settings, Set Up Layout and Navigation		
Add Functions and Features		
Develop and Add Content		
Add Images		
Implement Search Engine Optimization Plan		
Set Up Analytics, Marketing and Traffic-Building Plan		
Set Up Advertising, Affiliate Marketing and/or eCommerce Systems		
Set Up Systems to Maintain and Protect Site		
Plan For Your Future		

Website Tools
Choosing Domains, Hosting and Software

Checklist: Choosing Your Website Tools

Before you can set up your site, several important decisions must be made about the tools you will use. In this section, we'll cover these steps:

- ☐ Brainstorm Potential Domain Names

- ☐ Determine Your Webhosting Needs

- ☐ Select a Web Host

- ☐ Decide if You Will Use the Same or Different Companies for Domain Registration and Webhosting

- ☐ Register a Domain

- ☐ Purchase Webhosting

- ☐ Assign Your Domain to Your Webhosting Account

- ☐ Set Up Email

- ☐ Choose and Install Website Software

Domains

A "domain" is your address on the internet. It consists of your website name, preceded by "www." and followed by a "top-level domain", such as .com, .net or .org. Domain names are not case sensitive, so, while they appear on the internet in lower case, you can capitalize names within them in marketing materials to make the URL easier to read and remember. (For instance, whether you type www.youcanstartawebsite.com or www.YouCanStartAWebsite.com into your web browser, you'll end up in the same place.)

If you don't already have one, you'll need to buy and register a domain name. It usually costs $10–14 a year to register the domain name. You can buy a domain name from a webhosting company (see "Webhosting" for recommendations). In fact, I suggest deciding where you will host your website before you buy your domain name, as many webhosting companies will include the price of the domain in your webhosting package for at least the first year. You can search for availability of names on their sites.

Choosing a Domain Name:
- Choose a name that tells what your site is about or your name or company name.
- If you can, include "keywords" that potential visitors would use in searching the internet for what you have on your site. (See "SEO: Search Engine Optimization" for keyword research resources.)
- Generally, shorter is better. It should be easy to remember and easy to spell.
- Go for a ".com" site, unless your site is for a nonprofit organization or service, in which case, use ".org". ".Net" is next best, but anything other than .com or .org can make it more difficult for users to find you, unless you have a specialized use, such as ".tv" for a TV show.
- Avoid using hyphenated names. Like-this.
- If you are able to get a ".com" domain and are serious about your venture, consider also buying the ".org" and ".net" versions to prevent the potential confusion that could be caused if another organization used a similar domain address.

Buying a Domain Name
Before you buy your domain name, I suggest deciding where you will host your site and whether you will register the domain through the same company or a different one.

Options
Purchasing Domain and Hosting Together: I personally like the simplicity of keeping everything in one place. I now do this for most sites, purchasing everything through BlueHost, which is one of the web hosts I recommend. There, as with most webhosting companies, the domain is included free for the first year when you sign up for a hosting package. Another recommended web host, DreamHost, provides the domain free, as well as WHOIS privacy, with the purchase of a hosting package.

Purchasing Domains and Hosting Separately: Some website experts suggest buying your domain name and webhosting through separate providers, however, because:

- Separate providers may present cost savings or special features for certain types of users. For instance, users with a lot of domains may find GoDaddy's bulk rate plans to be cost-effective. Affiliate marketers also like a feature GoDaddy has that allows them to "mask" affiliate links. NameCheap is … pretty cheap overall, plus it gives free WHOIS privacy protection the first year and at a very low rate thereafter.
- If you decide to change hosting companies in the future for any reason, the transfer process is a little smoother if you only have to transfer the hosting and not the domain as well.
- While most webhosting companies provide one free domain for at least the first year when you sign up for a webhosting package, if you want to buy extra domains (for instance, the ".net" or ".org" version of your domain, in addition to the ".com" version), you might find special deals with lower rates for at least the first year.

Make sure to choose a reputable company. The companies I am mentioning here are ICANN-accredited registrars. They register the name for you, but you own it.

Keep good records and either make a note of when your domain is up for renewal or put it on an automatic renewal system. (If you place it on automatic renewal, make sure your credit card info is up-to-date!)

More Choices

When you sign up for a domain, you will be offered several options.

- **Length:** If you buy the domain for a longer period, the price per year may go down a bit. If you are just starting out, I suggest just buying it for a year.
- **Privacy:** When you buy a domain, your information (name, address, email, phone) is visible in a "whois" search. For a fee, generally about $10/year, you can make this information private.

Security

For security, unless you are in the process of transferring your domain, keep "Lock Status" on "locked" so it cannot be transferred away.

Choosing Domain Names

Domain Name Strategy

When choosing a domain name, look for one that ...

- Clearly describes your site, product or organization
- Is as short as possible
- Is easy to remember
- Is easy to spell
- Includes words a prospective visitor would use in an internet search

Step 1: Determine Key Words

If you are able to use your own name, your organization's name or your trademarked name, that can be an ideal domain name. (And conversely, or course, avoid using or incorporating others' names or trademarks.)

Generally speaking, it's best to keep your domain name as short as possible. At this point, most powerful one-word names have been taken, at least the ones with the most powerful top-level domains, such as .com. Look for possible combinations using a second word (and a third word if necessary). Consider words that are specific and descriptive and those that will set your name apart. (For instance, add your location or specialty.) Also consider short descriptive phrases.

The Single Most Important Word to Include:

Second Word Options:

Third Word Options:

Short Phrase Options:

Words (or Phrases) Visitors Would Use in a Search:

Step 2: Generate Options

Now, play with various combinations. List many possibilities. You can do this on a web host's site, as well. Most will suggest variations if the exact domain you want is already taken. I suggest you play with this yourself first, though.

Brainstorm domain names here:

Step 3: Select Good Options

Next, select several good options. Consider checking the words or phrases with SEO Keyword tools to determine search volume for your terms. Also consider trying them out with trusted friends who can give you feedback. List your favorites in priority order.

Step 4: Check Availability and Refine

Then check availability of your preferred names. Refine your choices, if needed, considering Keyword research, as well as options suggested by your domain provider and friends.

Step 5: Purchase Your Domain

Be prepared to purchase your preferred domain without too much delay. It can be very disappointing to go back later and find that the name you loved has been taken.

Webhosting

A web host is where your website lives. There are many options and checking them out can be confusing. I have tried several and have found that what matters most to me are:

1. Reliability (including "up time", speed and security)
2. 24/7 Customer Service
3. A good record with WordPress, the free content software I recommend

Of course, cost matters as well, but saving a little money is not worth a tradeoff of these critical requirements. If you need specific features, look for those, but most of the major services are feature-rich — most individual users probably won't need all of the features offered.

My current recommendations are:

BlueHost: I've used BlueHost for several sites and, based on my experience, have naturally recommended them to others. Historically, their customer service people have been very good — this is extremely important when you have issues and questions (especially late at night). They are one of the hosts WordPress consistently recommends. First year of domain registration is included with your hosting plan.

FatCow: For small businesses and individuals who value customer service, an interesting alternative is FatCow. In addition to boasting highly-rated US-based phone support, promoting attractive rates and radiating a sense of fun (check out their "HeiferCratic Oath"), FatCow is powered 100% by wind energy.

HostGator: Another popular award-winning host. Their "Hatchling Plan" provides a relatively inexpensive way to get started. (Note: You can only host one domain/site on the Hatchling Plan. If you plan to put up additional sites, consider the "Baby Plan".)

DreamHost: A host also recommended by WordPress. Their hosting plans includes domain registration and WHOIS privacy. DreamHost offers free webhosting to nonprofit 501(c)(3) organizations registered in the US. They are employee-owned and have been recognized by WorldBlu as one of their "Most Democratic Workplaces" from 2008–2013.

Tips:

- "Unlimited sites" means that you can host multiple sites on one account and only have to pay for the additional domain names (i.e. you don't have to pay extra to host the additional domains).
- Consider how you will back up your site. Stuff happens. Web hosts may provide a back-up service free or for an additional fee. If you have a lot of content and/or are changing it frequently, this option may provide ease and peace-of-mind. Check the fine print, though — even the best hosts may not entirely guarantee their backup, so if you want to be sure of backing up your site, it would be wise to supplement their backup procedure with other automatic back-up options. (See "Protecting Your Site".)
- Generally, the price per month for hosting goes down as you commit to longer time periods. There is often a discount for the initial period and the price goes up when you renew your plan.

Webhosting: What Do You Need?

Take a few minutes to explore your needs related to webhosting. Based on the answers to these questions, what capabilities will you require?

Webhosting Decisions

I plan to create:

- ☐ *Just one website or blog*

- ☐ *More than one website or blog*

- ☐ *Not sure yet*

If you think you may want to put up more than one website or blog, choose an "unlimited domains" webhosting plan.

I plan to create:

- ☐ *A static website*

- ☐ *A blog*

- ☐ *A website with a blog*

WordPress makes it possible to create both websites and blogs. If you plan to use another software, such as a web host's "simple drag-and-drop" software, and hope to blog, check to be sure it has that capability.

How many email addresses do you envision needing?

Is it important to you to keep your domain registration information private?

If so, be ready to pay up to $10–15/year for Domain Privacy, or chose a web host that includes it in your package.

Do you plan to back up your website regularly?

Some web hosts offer regular back-ups (Check the fine print for details and costs). I recommend having a supplemental back-up plan, though.

Do you want to buy your domain and webhosting from the same provider?

What else is important to you when choosing a web host?

Webhosting: What is All of This?

When you go to purchase webhosting, you may see many unfamiliar terms in the host's marketing copy. If you have a large organization, complex or unusual needs, or are concerned for any reason, do get specific advice. For most beginners and small organizations, the recommended hosts' least expensive or next-least expensive packages will likely be sufficient (typical range: $4–15/month). (Most hosts will allow you to upgrade later and most have some sort of short-term guarantee. Check this out if you are uncertain.) Also, note that hosts often also promote "features" that are really promotional offers or upgrade services from third parties, such as Google or Bing advertising or shopping cart services.

I've tried to simplify the webhosting decision here by not getting too technical. If you're curious, though, here is a basic translation of some of the terms you'll see:

Shared Server: A "server" is the hardware and software system that provides network service. A "shared server" is one on which many websites reside (vs. having a "dedicated server", which may be needed for large volume or non-standard situations).

Linux: Linux is a standard operating system.

Most personal and small business websites use shared webhosting on a Linux platform. Most good web hosts these days offer "unlimited disk space" (storage space) and "unlimited bandwidth" (data transfer).

MySQL: This is database software that stores blog posts and functionality.

PHP: This is a programming language.

PHP page and MySQL databases are required for content management systems such as WordPress to work. (*Look for WordPress capability.*)

FTP: File Transfer Protocol, needed to transfer files from one host to another over the internet (i.e. needed to upload files).

cPanel: a popular management interface

You'll see all these and more. Don't be overwhelmed or intimidated. Look for reliability, WordPress, and 24/7 customer service.

Setting Up Webhosting

Connecting Your Domain and Website

Once you have both your domain and webhosting, you'll need to assign the domain to the hosting service. Follow your web host's directions for this. (An example of BlueHost's domain assignment process is shown below.)

If the domain is not registered with your web host, you'll be asked to verify ownership.

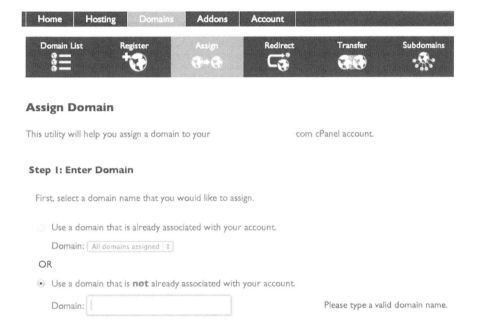

Email Set-up

One of the first things you'll want to do is to set up email addresses using your domain name (for example, yourname@yourdomain.com and/or info@yourdomain.com). The exact set-up process will vary depending on your host and email services.

Most hosting accounts give you the capability of creating multiple email addresses with your domain name. To simplify things, you may want to set up "Forwarders" to forward mail from these accounts to the email address you check most regularly.

For example, here is the section of BlueHost's control panel that allows you to create email accounts, along with forwarders and autoresponders.

Website Software

Unless you truly need a very simple site, I recommend using WordPress as your content management system.

Why I Like WordPress

It seems like every webhosting company is now promoting their free "simple" drag-and-drop software. *Sign up now and you can have your site up and running this evening.* Uh huh. I've tried several. What I found was that, while some were, in fact, fairly easy to use, they were only appropriate if you wanted a very simple site, because they only allowed for a few pages with basic features. Additional pages and upgraded features were available for additional fees. So it no longer ended up being "free".

Other software options I considered were expensive and required a lot of learning time.

I chose and recommend WordPress because it is 1) Free, 2) Feature-rich and 3) Popular. With the large and quickly growing volume of users (now more than 66 million), there are many features, "widgets", tools, and "plugins" available to enhance your site at little or no cost. While it does require a little effort to learn, it's fairly easy, and I believe the effort will pay off in the long-run.

The web hosts I recommend (and most others today) make it easy to install and use WordPress.

Note: WordPress has two versions and this can be confusing. One, www.wordpress.**com**, is available free for personal blogs and requires no additional webhosting fees. If you chose this, your site address will include "wordpress.com", unless you pay an upgrade fee for a customized domain name. WordPress may also run ads that will be seen by visitors who are not logged in (unless you pay a "no ads" upgrade fee).

If you want to put up a commercial site or use a customized URL, as most will, you will want the version from www.wordpress.**org**. You can sign up for a free account and download it there, or install it simply through your webhost.

Install WordPress:

- Go to your webhosting account cPanel (http://yourdomain/cpanel). Look for WordPress or a "one-click" or quick install option. If you need help, follow your hosting company's directions. For example, on BlueHost's cPanel, you can install WordPress by clicking on either WordPress under Website Builders or OneClick Installs under Mojo Marketplace.

Bluehost cPanel

- Indicate the domain on which you wish to install WordPress.
- If you are on BlueHost's Mojo Marketplace for your install, check "Advanced Options" and your screen will look like this.

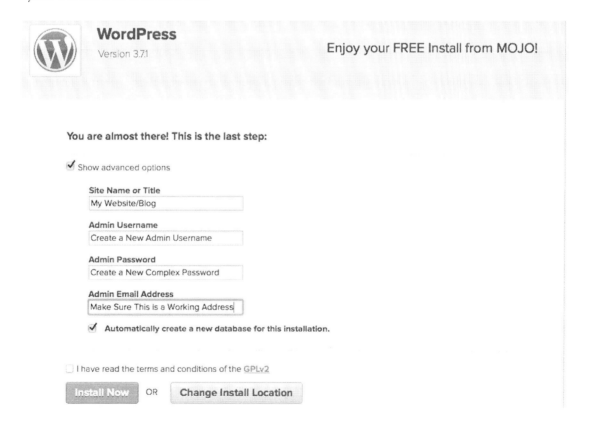

- Enter your Site Name, a new Admin Username and complex Admin Password. (Be sure to record these on your "Website Record" worksheet.) Be sure that the Admin Email Address you have entered is a working email. Agree to the terms and conditions and then install.

- Sign in to WordPress at *http://yourdomainname.com/wp-admin* or through WordPress on your host's cPanel.
- Important: For security reasons, do not use the default "admin" as your Username. If you did not change the Administrator Username and Password already through "Advanced Options" or another means during the installation, you'll want to create a new more complex Username for yourself in the "administrator" role. To do this:
  - ‣ On the WordPress Dashboard, scroll down to find "Users" in the left-hand column. Click on that and then "Add New". Enter your new Username, your email address and a strong password. Designate the role as Administrator.
  - ‣ To delete the old default administrator, "admin", you'll have to log-in again using the new administrator Username and password. Follow directions very carefully when you do this, or you may inadvertently delete existing content if there is any. Go to Users/All Users. Both your new and default "admin" administrator Users should appear. Delete the old default "admin" Username, following the directions precisely, checking "Attribute old posts to new account" so you don't delete them. If you are unsure of how to do this, get some help with this step.
- Important: For security reasons, be sure to also create and use a Nickname different from your new Admin Username and change "Display Public" to that name. Do this under Users/Your Profile in the left-hand column.
- Carefully record all of your Usernames and passwords and store them on your Website Record worksheet.

Just Need Something Super-Simple?

I have become a big fan of WordPress. It does, of course, require some investment of time and energy to learn. The payoff is a great deal of flexibility and availability of huge variety of features.

If you truly need something very simple — for example, a 1–5 page static (i.e. without blogging) informational site with a basic design and few features — some simpler alternatives may be appropriate.

Most webhosting companies have some sort of "simple" website builder available. Some of these have more capabilities than others. If you're considering this route, check out the free Weebly drop-and-drag software, available in BlueHost's, FatCow's and HostGator's hosting packages. It is simple and intuitive — the free version allows for up to six web pages and can accommodate photo galleries, audio, video and other features. You can try a "demo" on BlueHost's site.

SimpleSite is a service that packages the whole process of domains, hosting and software together. It does simplify matters, while trading off some design flexibility. A domain name using their URL — www.yoursite.simplesite.com — is provided free. You can obtain your own domain name for an extra fee. Both SimpleSite and another website packager, SquareSpace, provide free trials so you can check their products out before paying.

Now you're ready to set up your site.

Setting Up Your Site

Checklist: Setting Up Your Site

WordPress presents endless possibilities. Here, I'll give you some quick general tips and suggestions to get started. As you work with WordPress, you'll learn more about its capabilities and make the specific adjustments that are best for your particular site. You can find good detailed directions and help at www.wordpress.org/support.

Checklist: Setting Up Your Site

- ☐ Familiarize Yourself With WordPress

- ☐ Install a WordPress Theme

- ☐ Customize WordPress Settings

- ☐ Add Pages or Posts

- ☐ Set up your Layout and Navigation

- ☐ Add Features and Functions with Plugins

- ☐ Add Images

WordPress Orientation

First, get familiar with WordPress.

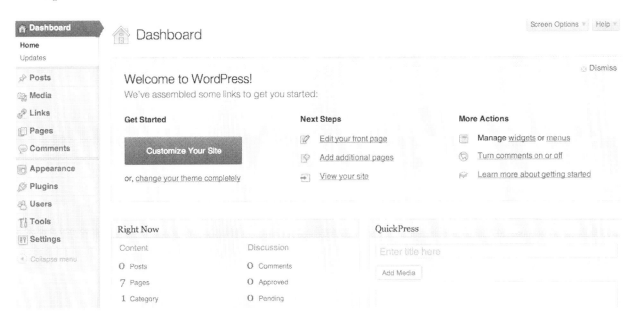

On the Dashboard, in addition to links to first steps and common actions, you will see a summary of "Right Now" Content and Discussions on your site.

Look at the navigation on the left-hand side of your screen. We'll cover each menu item in detail later, but for now just play with each item one at a time:

Posts: WordPress is set up for blogging. This is where you will add and organize blog posts.

Media: You can upload and edit photos, audio and video here.

Links: If you want to link to other sites, you can add links here.

Pages: This is where you will do most of the work for a standard website. You will add, format and organize your website pages here.

Comments: If you have a blog, you can view, approve, edit and delete comments you've received here.

Appearance: This is an important section where you can manage your Themes and Menus, as well as Widgets.

- **Themes:** One of the great things about WordPress is that you can easily change the overall look simply by changing the theme. You can install themes here, preview how they will look, and then activate your choice. Some themes have custom settings which can be adjusted under "Theme Options". For example, some themes allow you to make adjustments to the background color, header, footer, or sidebars.
- **Menus:** This is where you will organize your navigation and pages.
- **Widgets:** WordPress themes come with a variety of "widgets" built in that can add features and content to your sidebars, such as a search form, a calendar or list of recent posts. You simply drag the widgets you want into the sidebar.

Plugins: You can also add all sorts of features and functions to your WordPress site by adding Plugins. For instance, you can add buttons to share your content on various social media outlets, add standard forms or search engine optimization tools.

Users: This is where you manage user profiles and can give other users permission to write, edit, contribute or alter content.

Tools: "Import" allows you to import posts or comments from another system. "Export" allows you to export and download an xml file you can then use to import into another WordPress installation.

Settings: Under "General" you will set up your site title and general settings. Under "Writing", "Reading", and "Discussion", you will decide how content will appear.

WordPress Themes

The "theme" provides the basic look, design and functionality of your site.

On your WordPress Dashboard, go to "Appearance" and then "Themes". WordPress comes with a default theme, such as "Twenty Thirteen", which you will see there under the "Manage Themes" tab.

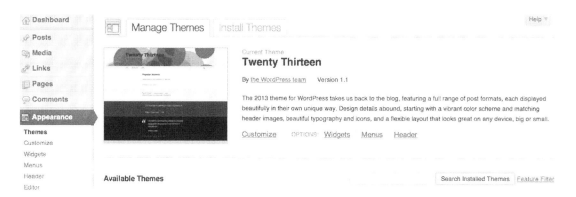

WordPress provides many free themes with different backgrounds and designs, along with upgraded paid versions with more features. Click on the "Install Themes" tab and you can search for other themes that meet the criteria you designate with the "Feature Filter".

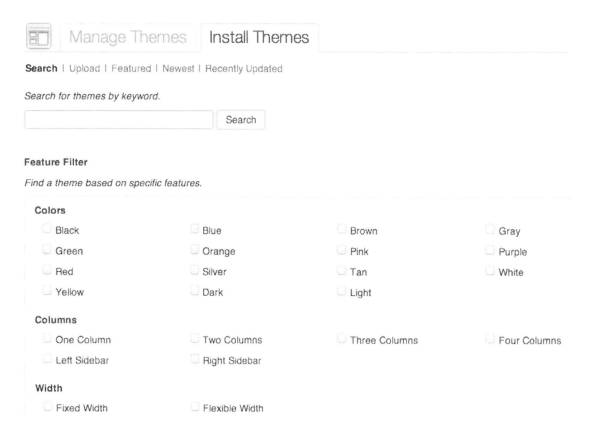

You might experiment a bit and choose a couple of different themes to try out. When you install additional themes, they will appear under the "Manage Themes" tab. You can then click on "Live Preview" to see how your site would appear using each theme. When you find one you like, you can click on "activate" and your site will now appear with that theme's backgrounds and features. For the most part, you can switch themes in and out with a click to see the different designs without messing up your content. (I recommend having a back-up just in case, though.)

Note: Your content may appear differently when you switch templates because of the template format itself. Also, if you have altered the template code, you will lose those changes.

If you need or want something more than one of the free themes offers, such as a particular "look" or a theme designed for a specific purpose (ex. a magazine or eCommerce template), many themes created for use with WordPress are available for purchase. These can give your site a much better appearance and many nice features at a very reasonable cost. Most also offer some level of support. (Note: It is possible to add many features to WordPress with free plugins and it is possible to add other nice design elements if you know html code, but much of this can be simplified with an inexpensive template.)

$30-50 Budget

I have used and was happy with templates purchased from ThemeForest, where you will find hundreds of WordPress themes for around $30–50.

If you want to experiment with themes, another option I've liked is ElegantThemes, which offers a portfolio of more than 80 WordPress themes for an annual membership fee of around $40.

$60-90 Budget

For a slightly larger investment ($60–80), a good choice for many would be a theme from StudioPress. Known for security, built-in content optimization and support, StudioPress creates a variety of theme designs all based on its foundation Genesis "framework".

Another good option around $90 is Thesis from DIYthemes LLC. Experienced web designers choose it for its search engine-optimized, fast-loading theme framework, as well as its Visual Design Template Editor.

"Drop and Drag"

Lastly, if you have a slightly larger budget and want more "drop and drag" type design flexibility, you could add a plugin to a good basic theme — for instance, use the Visual Composer plugin ($25) with StudioPress' Genesis theme, or use ElegantThemes' Builder Plugin with one of their themes ($89 Developer annual membership includes access to more than 80 themes and all of their plugins).

Or try creating your own themes with a "drag and drop" software such as Artisteer. (A free trial is available on their site.)

Choosing a Theme

Sorting through theme options can be overwhelming. To simplify the process:

- Decide on a **type of theme**. For instance, do you want an "eCommerce" theme, a "magazine" theme, a "corporate" theme, or a "creative" theme to show off your portfolio? Do you plan to "blog"?
- Consider the **basic design** that will work best for you. For example, do you want right-side or left-side sidebars? Do you want a customized "header", for instance, or a photo "slider" at the top? Do you want certain colors? Do you want a certain number of columns?
- Identify the **features** you really need, as well as those that would be "nice to have".
- Because users are more frequently viewing sites on tablets and other mobile devices, I highly recommend choosing a **"responsive"** theme that will adjust the page based on the screen on which it's being viewed.
- If you go shopping for a theme on a larger site with themes from many different designers, such as ThemeForest, go to the page that has your desired type of WordPress template. Start by limiting your choices to templates that are both highly rated and have at least fairly high sales volume. Every new product will have a few bugs, so you want one on which most of the bugs have already been eliminated. The more users there are, the more likely that the bugs have been fixed and that the developer will provide decent support. Sort through the options to find ones with your desired features.
- You can then check out the look and features through a "live preview" or "screen shots".
- After you purchase the theme, download it and follow the provider's directions to install it. (Generally, you will find a zip file to upload the theme file to your WordPress account. Sometimes Mac users will have to go to their Finder menu and Compress the file to create a zip file.) On your WordPress dashboard, go to the "Appearance" tab and find "Themes". At the top of the "Themes" page, click on the tab that says "Install Themes". Click on "Upload" to upload the theme. Then click on it to activate it.
- Themes generally come with at least a few "Theme Options" that allow you to customize elements such as the background colors, sidebar, headers and footers. After you install it, adjust the settings for your theme as desired. For instance, create a Customized Header with your logo or selected image.

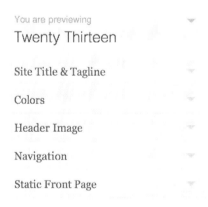

WordPress "Twenty Thirteen" Theme Options

Use the following worksheets to help you make theme decisions.

Theme and Tool Decisions

What do you need your site to do? Choosing a theme can streamline your design process.

Themes come with pre-formatted templates for different page layouts. They may also provide "Shortcodes", pre-coded design elements, such as Buttons, Tabs, "Sliders" (ability to create a slideshow), Columns, or Lists. Some include pre-formatted pages for common formats needed for different types of sites — for example, some are set up automatically to allow you to easily add a Gallery, Price Chart, Reviews or Team profiles.

Theme vendors offer specific type of themes in categories such as Corporate, eCommerce, Magazine, Blog, Multimedia, Creative, Personal, or Nonprofit. Within these, you can even find themes available for very specific needs, such as for a church or band, photography business, or restaurant.

Here are some questions to guide you through choosing a theme.

Site Type
My site is primarily this type:

- ☐ Corporate
- ☐ eCommerce
- ☐ Magazine
- ☐ Blog
- ☐ Multimedia
- ☐ Creative
- ☐ Personal
- ☐ Other

Design/Layout
I envision a layout with:

- ☐ Full-width pages
- ☐ 2 Columns
- ☐ 3 or more Columns
- ☐ Right Sidebar
- ☐ Left Sidebar
- ☐ Responsive Layout (recommended) (i.e. page adjusts to size of screen)
- ☐ Color(s):
- ☐ Customized Header

Navigation/Menus

The site will be organized with:

- ☐ Primary Navigation in Header only
- ☐ More than one Navigation (ex. Footer also)
- ☐ Drop-down Menus

Functions and Features

What other functions do you need on your site? Here are some examples of elements that may come built into your theme, but might also be added with a Plugin.

Layout Features

- ☐ Slider (slideshow)
- ☐ Portfolio or Gallery
- ☐ Pricing Charts
- ☐ Reviews
- ☐ eCommerce
- ☐
- ☐

Functions

- ☐ Social Media Connection
- ☐ Contact Form
- ☐ Maps
- ☐ Site Back-up
- ☐
- ☐

Additional Services

Some functions can be accomplished with Plugins, but may be best handled by incorporating outside services.

- ☐ Shopping Cart
- ☐ Mailing List sign-up and management
- ☐ Events Management
- ☐ Membership Groups
- ☐ Site Back-up
- ☐

Theme Options

As you explore options for your website theme, keep track of your top choices here. Note where you found them, the price, the key features and any potential issues, such as additional features you want that aren't provided by the theme. (You may be able to add some desired features with a Plugin.)

Theme:

Source:
Price:
Features:

Potential Issues:

Additional Notes:

Theme:

Source:
Price:
Features:

Potential Issues:

Additional Notes:

Theme:

Source:
Price:
Features:

Potential Issues:

Additional Notes:

Theme:

Source:
Price:
Features:

Potential Issues:

Additional Notes:

Setting Up WordPress

When you first install WordPress, you'll be faced with many choices. Don't be overwhelmed. You can change most settings later as you get some experience with your site and visitors. I'll guide you through some of the key ones below — a few of the most important ones have been bolded.

Note: When you make changes to your settings or content, be sure to click on "Save" or "Update" before moving on.

First, on your Dashboard, go to Settings.

General Settings:

⚙ Settings

General
Writing
Reading
Discussion
Media
Permalinks

- **Enter your Site Title and Tagline.** These are important, as they show up at the top of your website and in the description when your site shows up in Google (or other) searches. If possible, incorporate some Keywords potential visitors would use in searching for you in it.
- Don't change the WordPress Address and Site Address.
- Do you want anyone to be able to register to participate on your site? If so, it's suggested that you set the New User Default Role to "Subscriber". (You will be able to designate specific users as Administrators, Editors, Authors, Contributors as well.)
- Put in your email address, Time Zone, Date and Time Display preferences.
- When finished, save your changes.

Writing Settings:

- Skip this for now.
- Go back later, if desired and select Formatting options, Default Post Category and Update Services.

Reading Settings:

These settings determine how your site will appear to readers.

- **Front page displays:** WordPress's default is to have your blog show up on the front (Home) page. If you want yours to appear as a regular website, change that to a "static page".
  - On the Dashboard, go to "Pages". Click on "Add New". At the top of the page, enter "Home" as the title. Go over to the right and click on "Publish".
  - Go back to "Reading" under "Settings". Select the "static page" button and set the front page to your "Home" page.
  - If desired, add a "Blog" page following the directions above, and select that as your "Posts" page.
- Blog posts: To prevent long loading times, keep it to ten or fewer
- Syndication feeds: If you plan to display feeds from other sites, indicate the number you'd like shown (ex. up to 100).

- Blog feed appearance: Select whether you want to show the full text or just a summary of articles in the feed.
- **Search Engine Visibility:** If you want to be "found", make sure the box discouraging search engine indexing is UNchecked.

Discussion Settings:

Make your choices regarding discussions on your blog. For instance:

- Notifications: Do you want to notify any blogs linked to from your articles? (Probably, yes. It's an acknowledgement to the author giving them credit.) Allow link notifications from other blogs (pingbacks and trackbacks)? (Perhaps not.) "Pingbacks" and "Trackbacks" interconnect different blogs. A "pingback" notifies an author that someone has linked to their blog article. A "trackback" notifies an author that someone has written something related to their blog, even if there isn't a specific link to the article. (Note: This allows links from other sites to show up in your comments section. While this might sound good, spammers may use this for links to spammy sites. If spam becomes an issue, you may want to disable this.)
- **Allowing Comments:** Do you want to allow comments on all new articles? (If not, you can allow them on specific pages or posts later. See directions in the "Adding Pages" section.) Do you want to approve comments or a commenter before their post is shown? Do you want to receive an email when a comment is posted?

- Comments Format: Do you want to require the comment author to fill out their name and email or register? How many comments do you want to be displayed? Oldest or newest comments at the top? Do you want to receive an email when a comment is made? Do you want to approve comments before they show up on the site?
- **Comment Moderation:** You can hold comments for moderation that include words you specify or more than a certain number of links. This can help you cut down on spam on your site. (Suggestion: Hold comments in queue if they contain more than two links, as a common characteristic of spam is having a large number of links.) You can also "blacklist" comments that contain specified words.
- Avatars: Do you want to display an avatar image next to your name when you comment?

Media:

This sets the default sizes for images inserted into the body of your pages and posts. Suggested: Leave the defaults for now and alter them later if desired.

Permalink Settings:

This feature allows you to determine how the URL will appear for blog posts. This is an important factor in search engine optimization.

You can choose to leave the default, which will create a URL with a number in it, or your can choose from several other options which might include a date and a post name.

For best search results, choose URLs that appear as words. I suggest choosing *"Post Name"*, which will just show the title of your post, or *"Custom Structure"* with */%category%/%postname%/*, which will show the category as well.

(Note: Permalinks apply only to blog posts. For website pages, the URL will be *www.domainname/page-title*.)

Adding Pages and Posts

The process for adding WordPress Pages and for adding blog Posts is similar, so I'll start with adding pages as an example. Under the Pages Menu, you can Add New pages. Enter the Page Title at the top.

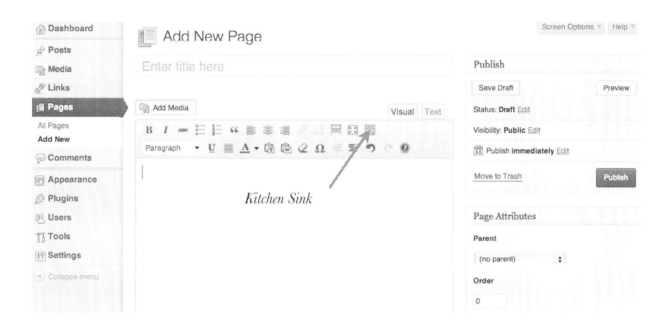

Formatting Tips:
- The Formatting bar appears at the top. Hover over each icon to see its function. If you click on the "Kitchen Sink" icon near the top right-hand corner, it will open up additional formatting options.
- You can paste in content created in another program, but formatting differences can cause issues. Your options are to paste in copy as plain text from Notepad (PC) or TextEdit (Mac) or use the "Paste from Word" icon, which will paste in content from Word without the formatting.
- Spellcheck your content before you paste it in to WordPress.
- WordPress allows you to enter content in visually, however, if you know html, you can also enter content with code using the "Text" tab.
- Adding a Link: Highlight the text you'd like to link, then hit the "Insert/Edit Link" icon in the Formatting bar. Enter the URL to link, along with a Title and designate whether you'd like the link to open a new window. (You will usually want a new window to open when someone clicks on the link, so that your page remains open.) You can also use this icon to link to another page on your site. After adding links, check them to be sure they work properly.
- If you are showing an email address on your website, hide it within a graphic to avoid excess spam and/or use a secure email contact form. (See the section on "Plugins".)

Publish:

This section on the top allows to you to control the visibility of your pages. You can Preview the page before you publish it. You can keep it as a Draft or designate it as Pending Review if you want an editor or other to review it before it's published. You can also designate whether the page will be visible to the Public, Password Protected, or Private.

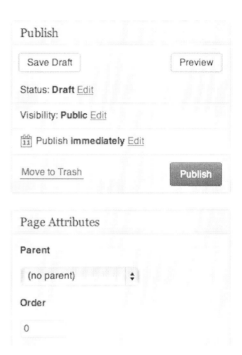

Page Attributes:

This section in the right column allows to you designate where and how the page will show up. You can identify a "Parent" page and a "Template" format. (For example, your WordPress template may give you the option of having your navigation on the side, or having a sidebar on the left or right). You also have the option of assigning a page number here. (If you don't assign a page number, under All Pages, your pages will show up in alphabetical order by Title.)

Comments:

If you haven't allowed Comments on all pages or posts (via your Discussion settings) you are still able to allow them on specific posts or pages. Under "Posts", go to "All Posts" or under "Pages", go to "All Pages". Click on "Quick Edit" and you can check a box that allows comments on that post or page.

What's Different with Posts: Categories and Tags

You can organize your blog posts with Categories and Tags so they can be more easily found by visitors and search engines. "Categories" would be similar to subjects in a book's table of contents and "Tags" comparable to entries in an index. These provide another opportunity to put in Keywords. To see how this works, under "Posts", go to "Add Post" and notice where you can indicate these on the right side. As you add categories and tags, they will show up in summarized version in the Dashboard under Posts/ Categories or Tags.

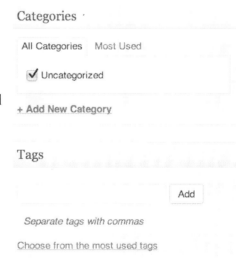

Now, add a few pages or posts, and then we'll work on the layout.

Setting Up Your Layout

Layout options will vary a lot depending on the theme you are using for your site. While I'll cover some basics here, you will likely have to experiment with your own theme. For instance, some will allow you to customize the background colors, style or layout.

Remember, one of the great things about WordPress is that you can change the theme with a click. (Caution — if you have altered the theme, you will lose those changes, or the new theme may not accommodate some of your customization or it may appear differently. It's a good idea to back up your work and/or document your alterations before experimenting with a new theme.)

Menus/Navigation

On your Dashboard, under Appearance, you will find the Menus menu, where you can set up your navigation. Some themes allow you to navigate using more than one menu. For instance, you might use a primary navigation and a footer navigation.

At the top of the Menu page, click on the + tab to create a menu. Then go over to the left side and check the pages that go under that menu and "add to menu". (If you have indicated a "parent" page when creating the page, it will appear indented under the "parent" on the list.) When the pages show up under the menu, you can then drag the names around to create the order you like and also drag names to the right to place them under another menu label on a "drop-down" menu. Then click on "save menu".

After setting up your Navigation, click through it on your site to be sure it works as intended.

Widgets

Your theme will include a variety of "widgets" that allow you to add features and content to your sidebars. You simply drag the widgets you want into the sidebar. For instance, you might drag the "Text" widget into the sidebar and then type in customized copy. (You can copy and paste in advertising code here, for instance.) Other common widgets for Blogs allow you to show Recent Posts, Recent Comments, an Archive, Categories, a Tag Cloud, an RSS Feed or a Search function in your sidebar.

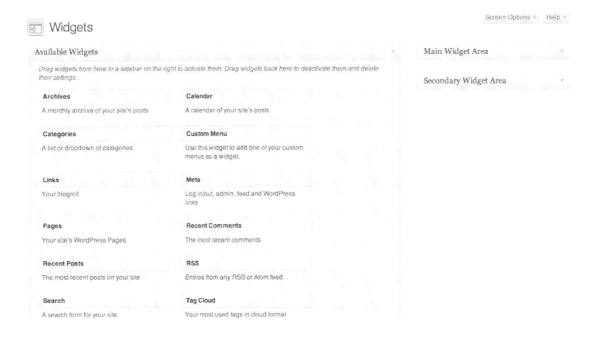

After you drag the widgets into the sidebar, you can drag them around to change the order. Some allow further customization, such as addition of a title. Experiment with these to obtain the look and functions you want. Some themes allow you to create different sidebars (or you can install a Plugin that will allow you to create additional sidebars). When this is the case, you indicate the desired sidebar for each page in a drop-down menu in the sidebar where you Add/ Edit Pages.

Adding Images

Images add life to the look of your site.

If you don't have your own photos, you can look for photos that are in the "public domain", purchase "royalty free" images inexpensively from online sources or even obtain some free if you obtain permission and/or credit the photographer and source.

"Public domain" means works are available for use without any copyright fees or additional permissions. This may be because the copyright has expired, because it didn't meet the requirements for copyright protection or because the creator has forfeited or donated the rights. Copyright length varies from country to country and depending on when the work was created, but generally it expires 50–70 years after the creator's death. Works created by the US government are considered to be in the public domain in the US. (There are always exceptions, so you should always check out the specifics for the work you are considering using and check with an expert qualified to give you a legal opinion if needed.)

"Royalty-free" means you can use copyrighted material you have paid for without needing to pay an additional fee every time you use it.

Free and Inexpensive Images

Here are some sources for free images. Be sure to read the detailed requirements for using their photos.

Morguefile.com has thousands of free high resolution photos that can be used in creative projects, but not as standalone product.

Wpclipart.com has free downloadable public domain clip art and illustrations.

Freedigitalphotos.net has thousands of images that can be used free in small sizes appropriate for a website if you acknowledge the creator and freedigitalphotos.net. If you do not wish to include the acknowledgment, the photos can be purchased for a few dollars apiece.

Stockfreeimages.com also provides small-sized photos that are free when you insert a credit line. (The "sister" site, www.dreamstime.com has thousands of additional low-cost photos available.)

Likewise, Stock.xchng®, www.sxc.hu, provides many free images in exchange for various types of acknowledgements, and also has a "sister" site, www.istockphoto.com with additional photos for purchase.

Wikimedia.org can also be a good resource for photos. Look for photos that indicate they are in the "public domain" or add the proper acknowledgment.

Graphics

If you'd like to create your own graphics, try free Gimp software to make graphics such as ads, website headers and social media backgrounds. Gimp Graphics Mojo is an inexpensive self-study video course that can help you get started.

Image Formats and Sizes

For websites, images need to be smaller than for print so that they will load quickly.

The formats used are JPG (jpeg), GIF, and PNG. JPGs are usually best for photos and images with a lot of color. GIFs are used for logos, line drawings, and other cropped images with transparent backgrounds. PNGs are less commonly used, but acceptable for both types of graphics.

Tips for Preparing Images for Websites:

- If you are using an image that will also be used for print, be sure to save a copy of the original image before editing it.
- Image sizes are measured in "pixels", with 72 pixels per inch.
- You may have to experiment with image sizes and resolution to determine the optimal balance between appearance and loading speed. Keep in mind that you want your pages to load as quickly as possible.
- Website Image Sizes: General Guidelines
  - Full-width (header banner): This may vary, but try to keep to 800 pixels or smaller.
  - Sidebar: 215 (with caption)–225 pixels
  - Center between sidebars: up to 470 pixels
  - Images used within page or post copy: 210–225 pixels
  - Headshots: 150–180 pixels
  - Thumbnails: Between 20x20 and 80x80 pixels
- Compressing Images: Some photos and graphics programs will give you options to automatically adjust the size of your photos for use on the internet. (ex. "Image Quality: Web" or "Optimize for Web"). If you don't have this, try a free online tool, such as Pixlr or Webresizer.
- Try to keep files to the following sizes:
  - High-quality photos: 100 KB or less
  - Multiple photos on a page: 50 KB or less each,
  - Banners and Headers: 60 KB or less

Adding Images

You can add images, audio or video to a page by clicking "Add Media" at the top of the page you are working on. You can then upload or drag in a file. This adds it to the Media Library. While it's probably best to resize, crop and adjust your photos before uploading them to WordPress, in the Media Library you are able to crop, rotate, flip and scale images. You can also add a Title, Alternative Text (text that is not normally visible to readers but may be displayed by web browsers when images are switched off and will be visible to search engines that don't "read" images), a Caption that will display underneath the image and a Description.

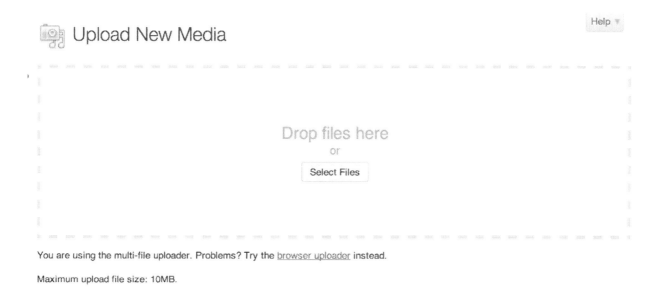

When you add an image to your page, you can also make certain adjustments. Click on the image and then on the small image icon in its top left corner and you can adjust the size, select the type of alignment, and add a Title, Alternative Text, Caption and Link. Under the "Advanced Settings" tab, you can add a border and further adjust size, spacing and links.

The "Title" will show up as text when the mouse hovers near the bottom of the image, the Caption will appear below it and the Link will open the designated URL when someone clicks on it.

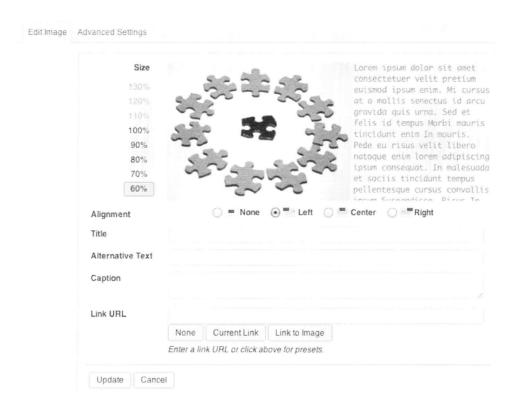

If you'd like to add a YouTube video, go to the video on YouTube, click "Share" and then on "Embed", copy the html code, then paste it into your page using the "Text" tab. When selecting the code to embed, YouTube allows you to adjust the size of the video screen. If you'd like to change the alignment, to center the video screen, for instance, you can do that by switching to the "Visual" tab in WordPress and making the adjustment there.

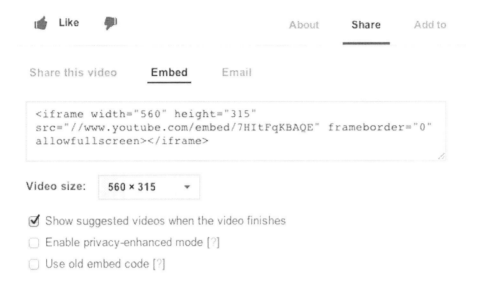

Or, to have a video open when a visitor clicks on text, when you are working on a page or post in WordPress, click on Add Media, then Insert from URL and fill in the desired Title text and URL.

Adding Functionality: WordPress Plugins

Basic Functions and Pages to Add

For most sites, the following additions are recommended (Depending on the purpose and scope of your site, you may need more or fewer.):

- Contact Form
- Sitemap
- Copyright notice
- Anti-Spam tools
- Search Engine Optimization
- Privacy Policy
- Terms & Conditions (disclaimers, policies, etc.)
- Social Media tools

One way to add these is with "Plugins".

A Plugin is a software extension that adds a feature to an existing software program. WordPress plugins can add all sorts of features to your site.

Using Plugins

Here are some tips for using Plugins:

- Start small. Thousands of plugins are available for WordPress. I'll suggest a few to start with. As you develop your site and content, you can explore more options.
- It's easy to go crazy installing plugins. Don't install more than you need, because they tend to slow down your site.
- Delete any that you don't use, have problems with, or find to duplicate others.
- Update plugins regularly.
- Look for plugins that are popular (have lots of downloads) and highly rated. They are more likely to get updated and provide support documentation.
- Only install plugins from trusted sources.
- Before installing, check for vulnerabilities. Make sure it will work with your version of WordPress. Always keep a backup of your site. Deactivate plugins if you suspect they may be interfering with other elements and functions of your site.
- You'll find lots of free plugins. Some have paid premium versions, but most of what you will need to begin with should be free.

To search plugin options, go to: Plugins and then "Add New".

- After choosing a plugin, click "Install" and then "Activate".
- After installing a plugin, don't forget to go into its "Settings" if needed to set it up as desired for your site.

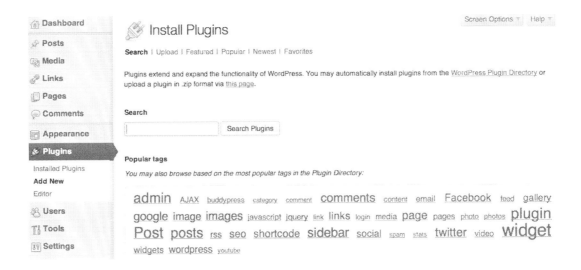

Popular Plugins

Here are some elements and functions to consider adding to your site, along with some possible plugins for the job. (Check them out for current information before installing.)

Contact Form: Make it easy for visitors to communicate with you, while hiding your email address from spammers, by using a contact form. Contact Form 7 and Fast Secure Contact Form are popular contact form plugins.

Search Engine Optimization Tools: When potential site visitors search online using search engines such as Google or Bing, you want your site to come up as early as possible in their search results. Search Engine Optimization ("SEO") tools consider how search engines work and what people search for online in order to help you strategically position your site to appear in as advantageous position as possible in search results. I use All-in-One SEO Pack by Michael Tobert, which allows you to put in a title, description and keywords for each page or post. Another popular SEO plugin is WordPress SEO by Yoast.

Sitemap: A sitemap is a list of pages of a website that helps search engine "bots" know what's on your site.

In earlier days, webmasters had to submit this information separately to individual search engines. Today, major engines such as Google, Bing, Yahoo and Ask all use web crawlers that identify pages. By creating and submitting a Sitemap, you can make it easier for them to discover all the pages on your site.

Google XML Sitemaps by Arne Brachhold is a popular Sitemap plugin. WordPress SEO by Yoast also includes an XML Sitemap.

Copyright Notice: Some themes will provide a way to add a copyright notice in the footer at the bottom of the page. If not, you can add a copyright notice to your site with a plugin, such as Copyright Proof, WP-Copyright-Protection or FooterPutter.

Anti-Spam Tools: To avoid as much spam as possible, consider using anti-spam tools. A popular one, Akismet, is still free for personal sites, but now charges $5/month for business sites. Additional options include: Antispam For All Fields, Invisible Captcha (for visitor comments), CryptX (to hide email addresses from spiders) and Really Simple CAPTCHA.

Legal Stuff: Websites typically include legal notices, such as a Privacy Policy, Terms & Conditions, and Disclaimer notices. You should obtain specific official legal advice from a qualified expert familiar with your situation on this.

It's likely that you will need to post a Privacy Policy, for instance, that notifies visitors of how their information will be recorded and used. While you may not be collecting information yourself, some of the internet services you use may be (Google, for instance).

Plugins are available that provide basic language you might be able to use as a starting point. For instance, WP-Insert provides "Set up Legal Pages" or you can try Easy Privacy Policy. If you use this sort of resource, note that you will still have to customize it for your particular situation. Again, be sure to obtain specific legal advice on this from a qualified professional.

Social Media tools: There are many plugins available to help you coordinate your site with social media sites, such as Facebook, Linkedin, and Twitter, as well as content sharing tools. Examples are: Share Buttons by AddToAny, which helps people bookmark, share and email your posts and pages using more than 100 different sharing and social bookmarking sites, Tweetable, which automatically tweets out your blog posts, and Facebook Like Button Plugin.

Website Backup: Popular free plugins to back up your site include WordPress Backup to Dropbox, BackupWordPress, BackWPup, UpdraftPlus Backup or XCloner. (If you use an automatic means of backing up your site, check it occasionally to be sure it's working properly.)

W3 Total Cache: This plugin is designed to improve the speed and user experience of your site.

Other Cool Tools

Broken Link Checker: Checks for and notifies you of broken links and missing images on your site.

Wp-Polls: Allows polling with visible results.

Disqus (pronounced "discuss"): Discussion community tool with features to organize comments and connect community members.

BuddyPress: Another community-building tool that makes it possible to create user profiles and groups.

WP Smush.it: Allows reduction of file sizes of the images on the site with minimal loss.

Free Plugins

Many good plugins are provided free. Their developers have likely invested much time and effort to make them available. If their products are useful to you, consider giving them a good review or even a donation.

Developing Your Website Content

Engaging Your Visitor

The Good News: With your website, you can reach more than 2.7 billion people around the world.

The Facts: There are more than 1 billion websites with more than 3.7 billion pages they can visit.

The Bad News: If you don't engage them within the first ten seconds or so of their visit, they are likely to move on to other sites and activities.

The Challenge: How can you keep your website visitor interested?

What do you want your website visitor to do specifically *while they are on your site?*

- ☐ Read
- ☐ Engage
- ☐ Share
- ☐ Decide to visit again
- ☐ Join
- ☐ Buy
- ☐ Contribute

Let's look at some strategies to increase the likelihood of your visitors taking these actions.

Read

What your visitor might be thinking as they land on your site: *Am I in the right place? Is this interesting? Is it worth my time?*

You have a short time to capture your visitor's interest.

Affirm that they're in the right place by making the benefit of your website clear. What is in it for them? Help them identify themselves in it. (*Oh, that's me they're talking to!*)

Capture their interest with good, unique, valuable content.

Respect their time by making the experience easy, easy, easy for them. Make it easy to find what they are looking for with clear navigation and a search function. Keep the most important content "above the fold" — that is, don't make them scroll down for it. Make it easy to read by using bullet points and white space to direct the eye.

Engage

Keep the visitor on your site by involving them. Use thought-provoking questions, assessments, discussions and surveys. When linking to other sites or pages, have a new page open so they stay on your site at the same time.

Share

What your visitors might be thinking when they consider sharing: *Is it unique? Do I believe it? Will this make me look good?*

Provide valuable, unique, well-presented content that others will want to share.

Make it easy for your visitors to share content with others by incorporating Facebook, LinkedIn, Twitter and other social media share buttons.

Visit Again

What your visitors might be thinking as they leave your site today: *Why should I come back to this website? Will there be something new? Something valuable? How will I know? How will I find it?*

Blogs are designed to continually provide fresh content. If yours is a regular website, consider ways to keep it fresh and up-to-date. Give visitors a reason to check back. For instance, update information, add new content, add a blog, or promote specials.

Make it easy for them to return by adding a bookmark, RSS feed or a "subscribe" button.

Join

What your visitors might be thinking when you ask them to sign up for a mailing list or "join" your community: *Why should I give this space in my already-cluttered inbox? What's the benefit? Will giving you my email address cause me to receive a lot more spam and junk mail?*

Make sure there's both an incentive for the visitor to give you their email address now (for example, a free resource guide) and an explanation of the added benefit they will receive by joining. For instance, will they receive extra content? Special rates? Preferential status? Timely notices? Easy access?

Conversely, how can they be assured that you won't flood their inbox with solicitations and junk? Certainly one of the reasons to collect email addresses is to be able to contact good prospects when you have something to sell. But too much of that is likely to drive them to the "unsubscribe" button. A good rule of thumb is to provide 80% content/value vs. 20% promotional material.

Buy

What your visitors might be thinking when they consider a purchase: *What do I need or want? Do I trust this source? Is it a good deal? Why should I act now? What if I make a mistake?*

Make it easy for your visitor to find what they want. Give your site a professional look and provide clear specific product information. Keep in mind that it is easy for internet shoppers to check out their buying options and be sure you are providing good value. Make sure it's easy to order and pay. Increase buyer confidence with a guarantee and/or easy return policy.

Contribute

If you want visitors to contribute to your community, make it easy for them. Pose questions. Encourage discussion. Invite comments and suggestions.

Your Three Audiences

When writing copy for your website, keep in mind that you are writing for three different audiences: Humans, Computers and Search Engines. This has implications for design, organization and language. Here are some tips for each:

Humans
- Design your site to draw your visitor in visually. Use color and interesting, appropriate fonts (generally no more than two). Use "white space" to make your site easy on the eye.
- Organize it clearly so they'll know where to find what they're looking for. Use headlines, bullet points and links to guide the reader.
- Use *their* language.

Computers
- Keep in mind how your content will appear on different types of screens. With the majority of internet users now viewing content at least some of the time on mobile devices, consider a "responsive" theme that adjusts content to the user's screen size.
- Keep the most important content near the top of the page so the reader doesn't have to scroll down to view it.
- Avoid using huge graphics and too many plugins that will slow down your site's loading speed.
- Check out your site on a variety of browsers. Currently Chrome, Firefox and Internet Explorer are the most-used browsers, with Safari and Opera also receiving notable usage.

Search Engines
- Incorporate "Keywords", words and phrases potential visitors would be using when searching for information, into your site, particularly in your titles, headlines and first paragraph copy on each page.
- Be sure to provide Titles and Alt Text for images.

Website Content: Finding the Words

Earlier we looked at defining the ideal visitors, or target audience, for your website — who your visitors are, their needs and wants and how they describe themselves. Look back at your responses. Now choose words that will connect with them.

First, let's look at the benefits of your site and offering *to your visitors*. What will they gain as a result of visiting or taking action there? Be sure to identify benefits, not just the features, of your site or product. (Test your answer by asking "so what"?)

Benefits You Provide to Your Visitors:

Then, consider how to connect what you have to offer with your target audience.

Words They Use to Describe Themselves:

What Your Visitors are Looking For:

Words They Use in Searching for Your Solutions and Benefits:

Incorporate these words and phrases into your titles, copy, headlines, and keyword tags (and domain name, if possible). Begin with the website Title and Description you will submit to directories, such as www.dmoz.org. If you use SEO tools such as the All-in-One SEO Pack plugin, enter these for your custom title and META description.

Title (maximum 60 characters)

Description (maximum 160 characters):

We'll work further with Search Engine Optimization Keywords in the Marketing section.

Writing for Blogs

To build a successful blog, you must build an audience. Keep this in mind in every aspect of your blog planning and writing.

Audience Building

Several aspects of your blog combine to make it attractive to visitors. Think about the blogs you like to read and share. It's likely that they demonstrate several of the following characteristics:

- Interesting Content
- Easy to Read
- Engaging
- Easy to Find
- Easy to Share
- New Content Added Consistently

Writing for Blogs: How Long and How Often?

Blog posts generally run between 250–800 words in length depending on the type of content.

As you plan your blog writing, keep in mind two factors: Continuity and Consistency

Tips for Continuity

- Each post should cover just one topic. You need not cover everything you have to say in one post!
- If you have a lot of content on a particular subject, plot out a series of posts.
- Keep in mind that you want your visitors to come back often. Give them a reason to come back for more.
- Use links within your posts to highlight and refer to previous related content.
- List Categories, Tags and Related Posts in sidebars or footers to make it easy for readers to find additional content of interest.

Tips for Consistency

- Post regularly. Search engines like new content. Each time you post, it increases your visibility. As a writer, you develop discipline and momentum. Your readers know what to expect and get in the habit of reading your posts on a regular basis.
- Before you commit to a regular post schedule, consider what will work both for you and for your readers. How often can you realistically produce good content? How often will you have something valuable to say? What are your visitors' habits? You need balance between momentum and burnout. It's hard to build an audience if you are not posting valuable content frequently enough for readers to stay engaged. And conversely, if you post too much, they may drop off because they can't keep up.
- Leave breathing room between posts for readers to engage. Give them a chance to comment and give yourself a chance to respond to comments.

Blog Writing Basics

Many of the basics of good blog writing are the same as for any type of good writing:

- Write with your specific audience in mind.
- Write clearly using precise language.
- Unless you're going for special effect, use good grammar. Use spellcheck and then proof your writing again.

Blog writing also requires specific attention to certain aspects of writing:

Write for Internet Readers.

Keep in mind that your blog will be read on screens. Since half or more of internet users are now receiving content via tablets and mobile devices, your content must show up well on smaller screens, as well as regular computer screens. Make it easy to read by using white space, headlines, visuals and bullets to guide the eye.

Write for Short Attention Spans

On the internet, you must grab attention fast or your visitor will move on. You'll need a good opening that makes them want to keep reading.

Write to Be Found and Forwarded

Use titles that will get attention from both humans and search engines. Keep in mind that your post title will be visible in searches, RSS feeds and on social media sites if your posts are shared. Make them search-friendly, descriptive, and attention-getting. When someone sees the title, will they want to click on it to find out more? Will they want to forward it on to others?

Write to Engage

Get your readers involved. If you want to encourage comments:

- Specifically ask for comments. (*Let me know what you think. I welcome your comments.*)
- Ask open-ended questions. (*What? How? Why?*)
- Ask provocative questions
- Ask for specific responses. (*Has this happened to you? Share your story. What advice would you give a friend in this situation?*)
- Interact with comments and you will likely receive more.
- Set a tone and example for how you want visitors to interact on your blog.

Managing Comments

Before you post content that allows, and in fact encourages, comments, have a plan to manage the process. It is likely that you will receive a mixture of both appropriate comments and inappropriate ones.

On the WordPress Dashboard under Settings/Discussion Settings, you can set up your Comment Moderation process. For instance, you can decide whether to require a commenter to register and you can choose to review comments before they appear. You can arrange to be notified by email when comments are made or when you need to approve comments. You can set up a "Comment Blacklist" to block out comments that contain certain words.

One of the big challenges with blog comments is dealing with spam. In an attempt to get higher search rankings, spammers often post comments with links to other sites (often inappropriate ones). Since comment spam often includes a large number of links, to cut out some spam, you can set your comments discussion settings up so that any comment containing a certain number of links (suggested: 2) is held for moderation before posting. Moderation does take time and attention, so take that into consideration in your planning.

To manage other types of inappropriate comments, consider posting a Comment Policy. For instance, state the types of comments that will be deleted by the moderator — obscene comments, plagiarized material, fake or anonymous comments, product promotion, personal attacks, etc. You can also ask readers to notify you of inappropriate comments.

Use the worksheets on the next pages to plan your blog strategy, brainstorm potential blog content and plot out a tentative blog calendar.

See "Building a Community Through Blogging" for more tips.

Blog Strategy

The Purpose of My Blog Is:

Who It's For:

How My Blog is Unique (why it will stand out among 250 million others in the blogosphere):

Potential Partners (ex. Collaborators, Guest Bloggers, Links, Feeds):

Potential Opportunities (ex. To be a Guest Blogger, for Links):

Blog Brainstorm

Depending on the purpose of your blog and your intended audience, blog posts can take many forms.

For instance, here is a list of types of blog posts to jog your thinking:

- ☐ News & Information
- ☐ Perspective on Current Events
- ☐ Predictions
- ☐ Opinions
- ☐ Reviews
- ☐ Resources
- ☐ Interviews
- ☐ Profiles
- ☐ Inspiration
- ☐ Practical Tools
- ☐ Humor
- ☐ Lists
- ☐ Stories
- ☐ Images
- ☐ Questions
- ☐ Contest
- ☐ Assessment
- ☐ "How To"
- ☐ Case Study
- ☐ Exercise
- ☐ Reader Challenge
- ☐ Reactions To Other Blogs
- ☐ Guest Posts
- ☐ Repurposed Material
- ☐ Series
- ☐ Audio or Video Clips
- ☐ Other

Brainstorm Potential Blog Topics

- Come up with as many ideas as you can. Go for 100.
- Right now, don't worry about whether they are good or not. Go first for quantity. You can evaluate, delete, modify, combine, or otherwise improve them later.
- Brainstorm by yourself first. Then try brainstorming with another person or a team.

Blog Topics and Content

Cull your list down to the best ideas here:

Did themes or patterns emerge?

How do these fit with your overall purpose and goals?

Now plot out a calendar of blog topics.

Blog Calendar

1st Quarter

    Goal:

    Theme:

2nd Quarter

    Goal:

    Theme:

Month 1:

Month 4:

Month 2:

Month 5:

Month 3

Month 6:

3rd Quarter

Goal:

Theme:

Month 7:

Month 8:

Month 9:

4th Quarter

Goal:

Theme:

Month 10:

Month 11:

Month 12:

Marketing, Money and Results

Website Marketing

By themselves, websites and blogs can achieve little. If you put up a website and don't do anything else, not much will happen. A few visitors may find you, but not many. Even if you add new content to keep your site or blog fresh and interesting, it won't produce results for you unless you undertake other marketing activities that work together with it to build traffic, audiences and conversations.

No matter what your purpose is for your website, you must attract the right visitors. The first step in this involves SEO, search engine optimization — taking steps to increase the likelihood of people finding you in online searches. If your site appears on page one of Google listings for your search terms, there's a good likelihood that a prospect may click on your site. But if you show up on page three or later, it's highly unlikely they will keep looking through the search results long enough to find you.

In addition to SEO tactics, there are several other steps you can take to build traffic to your website, as well as tactics to keep in touch with visitors to build relationships and encourage them to come back.

Lastly, you'll want to be able to analyze traffic to your website to see how well things are working, as well as the effects of adjustments you make.

Website Marketing Checklist

- ☐ Set up and Implement SEO

- ☐ Build Website Traffic

- ☐ Create Email Lists

- ☐ Obtain Links from Other Sites

- ☐ Contribute Content Through Articles and Participation in Blog Communities

- ☐ Evaluate Results with Website Analytics

SEO: Search Engine Optimization

Unless your site or blog is intended just for friends, you are probably interested in knowing about how to get your site to show up on the "front page" in Google searches.

The subject of Search Engine Optimization, or how to get search engines to recognize your site and rank it highly, is a complex one. While you may want to hire someone to help you with SEO or invest in some SEO tools, I'll cover some basics you can start with yourself at no cost.

SEO Basics

Search engines look for:

- **Keywords**: Use the words you think visitors would use in searching for what you have on your site. Use them specifically in:
  - Your Domain Name
  - Your Site Title
  - Your Site Description
  - Your Navigation Bar
  - Page Titles and Descriptions
  - Headings and Subheadings
  - First and last paragraph copy
  - Image Filenames, Titles, Alternate Text and Descriptions
- **Inbound Links:** Both quality and relevance count.
- **Fresh Content:** Refresh yours regularly.

SEO Tips

- Submit an XML Sitemap, a list of pages of the site, so that web crawlers can find your site's current pages. (The four biggest search engines, Google, Bing, Yahoo and Ask, all use the same protocol, so you no longer need to submit information to each one.) You can do this with a plugin, such as Google XML Sitemaps.
- Submit your site as well to the Open Directory Project, www.dmoz.org. ODP is a free website directory that powers core directory services for many other portals and search engines on the Web, including AOL, Gigablast, Lycos, Wisenut and hundreds of others. (You can check to see if you are in a directory by typing "site:yourdomain" into the search engine's search box.)
- You might also install an SEO plugin, such as the "All-in-One SEO" plugin, on your site.
- Add accurate descriptions and keywords to your pages, posts and images. Resist the temptation to overstuff them with keywords, though.
- Add value to your visitors' experience with rich content.

KeyWord ResearchTools

If you want to conduct some research to identify effective words and phrases, you have several options. You can pay a firm to do it for you, purchase SEO tools to do it yourself, or do some basic research with free tools. At the time of this writing, some of the free tools that are available are:

- www.ubersuggest.org: Enter a term and Übersuggest will suggest keyword ideas.
- Google Keyword Planner (Currently it is free, but you must establish a Google Adwords account at www.google.com/adwords.)
- www.semrush.com: While SEMrush sells a paid product, they have some useful free Keyword Research tools available on their site under the Tools and Analysis drop-down menu. For instance, you are able to see volume of searches for keywords, trends, and related searches, as well as get a feel for competition by examining the "CPC", cost-per-click, for keyword advertising.
- www.seobook.com: SEO Book provides several tools and a wealth of information when you sign up for a free account.

Use the following Keyword and SEO worksheets to develop and organize your SEO process.

Keyword Strategy

Page

Possible Search Terms	Volume	Competition

Page

Possible Search Terms	Volume	Competition

Page

Possible Search Terms	Volume	Competition

SEO Worksheet

Important places to use your Keywords on each page are:
- **Title**: This will be your Menu label. Use search keywords if possible.
- **Description**: This will be the copy that shows up in a search. (160 characters)
- **Paragraph Headings:** H1, H2 and H3 headings
- **Image Filenames** and **Alt Text** (alternative text associated with an image that appears when images are not available)
- **Categories and Tags**
- **Anchor Text (Link Label)** (the Title associated with a link. With some browsers, it is visible when hovering over the link.)
- **Content**: Use keywords naturally in the body text.

Use this worksheet to develop your Keyword strategy for each page.

Page
Title:
Description:
Paragraph Headings:
Image Filename/Alt Text:
Link Label:

Page
Title:
Description:
Paragraph Headings:
Image Filename/Alt Text:
Link Label:

Page
Title:
Description:
Paragraph Headings:
Image Filename/Alt Text:
Link Label:

Page
Title:
Description:
Paragraph Headings:
Image Filename/Alt Text:
Link Label:

Page
Title:
Description:
Keywords:
Paragraph Headings:
Image Filename/Alt Text:
Link Label:

Page
Title:
Description:
Keywords:
Paragraph Headings:
Image Filename/Alt Text:
Link Label:

Page
Title:
Description:
Keywords:
Paragraph Headings:
Image Filename/Alt Text:
Link Label:

Page
Title:
Description:
Keywords:
Paragraph Headings:
Image Filename/Alt Text:
Link Label:

Page
Title:
Description:
Keywords:
Paragraph Headings:
Image Filename/Alt Text:
Link Label:

Your Website's Place in the Marketing Circle

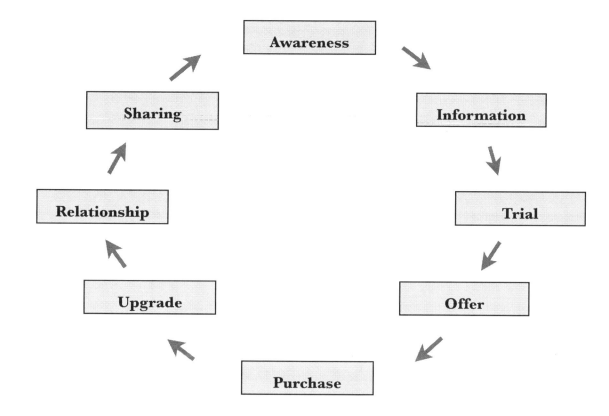

The role a website plays and other elements of the marketing circle vary according to the type of website.

For instance, consider a Brand-Building website or blog, such as a consultant or service professional might have. A prospect might find the website address from a business card, an online or trade magazine article, an ad or an online search. If the website is attractive, well-organized and relevant, they might stay around and look for information or check out an example of the website owner's work. Perhaps they will respond to an invitation or "call to action", such as a free trial or free sample in exchange for an email address. Then the website owner can connect further with newsletters or special offers to build a relationship, interest, and finally, a sale. If the buyer is happy, the marketing circle might expand with repeat or upgrade sales, as well as good "word of mouth" advertising or social media sharing.

A visitor to an eCommerce website might have arrived there as the result of an online search, an ad or some other type of marketing. If the visitor finds what they are looking for at a good price, they might purchase. Afterwards, they might respond to invitations to upgrade or repurchase based on their relationship history.

As you can see from these examples, it's not the website by itself that gets the result you want. The website is just one tool in the process of marketing. Other marketing elements and tactics before, during and after the website visit also are needed to produce the end result.

Consider your overall purpose. What role does the website play? Which other marketing tactics do you need to implement? For instance, tactics to:

Get Visitors to the Site

- ☐ Search and Directories

- ☐ Advertising

- ☐ Links from Articles

- ☐ Social Media Links and Feeds

- ☐ Links from Other Sites

- ☐ Email and Newsletters

Build a Relationship and Interest

- ☐ Subscribe To Email List or Join a Community

- ☐ Free Gift or Trial

- ☐ Blog Discussions

Inspire Action

- ☐ Special Offers

- ☐ Sharing Tactics

Building Traffic

Building traffic to your website is an ongoing process. In almost all cases, traffic builds over time as a result of consistent marketing activity.

Integrate your website into every aspect of your marketing.

Materials and Advertising: For instance, incorporate your web address into your:

- ☐ Email signature line
- ☐ Business cards
- ☐ Marketing materials
- ☐ Product copy
- ☐ Social media profiles

Writing: Add links to your website in your copy in:

- ☐ Articles and Press Releases
- ☐ Newsletters

Social Media: Connect with social media, using plugins to:

- ☐ Connect with your Facebook page and Twitter feed
- ☐ Automatically show new Posts on Facebook, LinkedIn and Twitter

Links: Seek out quality links from sites with relevant content.

- ☐ Directories (ex. www.dmoz.org, www.technorati.com, www.blogcatalog.com)
- ☐ Partnerships with other website owners
- ☐ Create content others will want to re-post. (Hint: "Top 10" lists, Resource lists and "Tip" or "Myths" lists are popular.)
- ☐ Create links back to your site by providing expert advice where appropriate on sites such as Squidoo, Google Groups or Yahoo Answers. (Follow their guidelines carefully.)

Blogging: Build interest through blogging:

- ☐ Guest post on other blogs
- ☐ Contribute comments to other blogs that get noticed — in a good way. Only comment where you can add value.
- ☐ Add an RSS button to your blog so readers can easily add you to their feed.

Mailing Lists

Would you like to be in touch with people who have visited your site? Perhaps you have a newsletter or would like to be able to share announcements, free information, notices of promotions, and such.

Websites often include an "opt-in" form where interested visitors can sign up to receive mailings and additional information. Even if you don't have an immediate plan to send out a newsletter or information, I recommend you include this so you are able to keep in touch with people interested in what you have to offer. It takes a while to build a list, a community, a relationship, so I recommend beginning this process from the start.

Email Requirements
There are two important laws to be aware of when you send mass emails.
- Opt-in: Your email recipients must have specifically agreed to receive email from you. You obtain their permission through an "opt-in" form.
- Unsubscribe: You must give them an opportunity to unsubscribe from your list.

List-Building Resources
Fortunately, there are good services that will manage your lists, and also provide resources that make it easy to create an opt-in form for your site, create newsletters, send email and even other marketing materials. I'll mention a few here, with pricing as of the time of this writing,.

Vertical Response is a good low-cost choice for beginners. You can sign up for a free account there to manage your list. They have a lots of short videos and resources to help you learn about lists, creating newsletters, email marketing and more. They also provide additional marketing services and products, including surveys, postcards, social media and event marketing.

With Vertical Response, if you decide to send out a newsletter or email, you can "pay as you go" by purchasing credits, just as you would purchase stamps. The cost depends on the volume you buy. For example, it currently costs $.015 each for up to 1,000 email credits or $.01 each when you purchase more than 25,000, and the price continues to go down from there. If you plan to mail regularly, you might consider a monthly plan, where you pay a flat fee based on the number of subscribers on your list. Plans currently start at $10/month for up to 500 subscribers ($8.50/month if you prepay for 12 months), $28/month for up to 2,000 ($23.80/mo. for 12 months prepaid), and so forth.

If you plan to send out email regularly, another good choice is Aweber. They will help you collect and manage your subscriber list, create newsletters, deliver an automatic series of emails with autoresponders, and track results. Their packages start at $19/month for a list of up to 500 subscribers ($49/quarter, $194/year). Aweber integrates with many third party applications, such as PayPal and E-junkie.

You may have heard of Constant Contact through their advertising campaigns. Constant Contact specializes in small business marketing. They offer email marketing services, as well as event and social media marketing services. Their rates start at $15/month for a list of up to 500 subscribers ($12.75/month with 12 months prepaid) and $30/month($25/month with 12 months prepaid) for a list of 501–2,500.

One other option is MailChimp. MailChimp offers a "Forever Free" plan that allows you to send up to 12,000 emails a month to a list of up to 2,000 subscribers. This plan doesn't includes some useful features available with their paid plans, though, such as autoresponders, "Time Warp" (the ability to deliver your email at a specific local time), "Delivery Doctor" and "Social Pro" (the ability to target campaigns to specific social media users), and MailChimp's badge shows up in your footers. Alternative plans include "Pay as You Go" plans: currently $.03 each up to 5,000 credits, $.02 each for 5,000–24,999 credits, then $.01 each for 25,000 or more credits. Monthly plans are available starting at $10/month for unlimited emails up to 500 subscribers, $15 for up 1,000, $30 for up to 2,500 and so forth.

Building Your List

Provide something free to encourage visitors to sign up for your list or "join your community". For example, you could give away a free report or a discount coupon.

To build a good, legal and responsive list, the "double opt-in" process is recommended. In the first step, the subscriber enters their email information on your opt-in form. In the second step, they receive an email asking them to confirm their subscription.

Keeping Subscribers

To keep subscribers, you must provide worthwhile information. Above all, you must keep from annoying them. It can be a delicate balance between sending emails consistently enough to remain top-of-mind and tempting subscribers to hit "unsubscribe" because your emails are too frequent or annoying.

While you certainly will want to be flexible enough to email your subscribers with truly timely and exciting news, consider plotting out a planned schedule. For instance, in addition to notifying subscribers whenever there's a new post on your blog, you might feature a special offer or newsletter on a specific topic monthly. Since you will be building your list over time, you may want to include popular recycled content, but make sure there is also always something new and valuable.

Most email services will allow you to segment your lists so you can target your emails and offers to subscribers' specific interests.

Use the worksheet on the next page to plot out your plan.

Subscriber Email Strategy

Month:	**Month:**	**Month:**
Subscriber List: Topics: Offer/Action:	Subscriber List: Topics: Offer/Action:	Subscriber List: Topics: Offer/Action:
Month:	**Month:**	**Month:**
Subscriber List: Topics: Offer/Action:	Subscriber List: Topics: Offer/Action:	Subscriber List: Topics: Offer/Action:
Month:	**Month:**	**Month:**
Subscriber List: Topics: Offer/Action:	Subscriber List: Topics: Offer/Action:	Subscriber List: Topics: Offer/Action:
Month:	**Month:**	**Month:**
Subscriber List: Topics: Offer/Action:	Subscriber List: Topics: Offer/Action:	Subscriber List: Topics: Offer/Action:

Building a Community Through Blogging

In addition to building direct sources of revenue, by building audiences for their content and traffic to their site, successful bloggers can increase their visibility and demand as speakers, writers, consultants and experts.

To build an online community, bloggers must provide valuable content and engage visitors. They can expand their community by making it easy for visitors to share content, by making content visible in feeds, and by actively posting appropriate content on other sites.

Provide Valuable Content

The most important factor in building a community through blogging is simply to provide valuable content. Create content that is interesting, relevant to your target audience and unique. Post regularly and give visitors a reason to return.

Engage Visitors

To get visitors to remain on and return to your blog, encourage comments and discussions. Get them involved by posing questions. Take surveys and provide results.

Simplify Sharing

Make it easy for visitors and potential visitors to find your blog and new content. Include subscription options on your site, both for RSS feeds and for email notifications of new content.

Set up automatic updating to link new content to your Facebook and other social media sites. This can be done with a plugin or through services such as Hootsuite or Onlywire.

Reach Out: Posting on Other Blogs

Bloggers are typically active not only on their own blogs, but on other blogs aimed at similar audiences. Commenting on other blogs is an art. If you want to start to participate in a blog community, it's wise to follow it for awhile and notice what is appropriate in that blog's culture.

Here are some general guidelines for commenting on other blogs:
- Contribute relevant information. Stay on topic.
- Acknowledge others.
- Provide something useful.
- Write comments of appropriate length — neither too long or too short.
- Use appropriate language. Don't write anything you wouldn't want to live on the internet for a long time.
- Don't blatantly self-promote or promote your product. If you do, you risk turning off other readers, as well as the blog moderator.

Build Community

Become visible in a larger community by connecting with other bloggers who serve similar audiences. For instance, you might include a Blogroll on your site. This is a list of links to other blogs readers might find of interest. It's usually located in the sidebar or footer.

If appropriate, mention other blogs in your posts and let the other bloggers know. A "Pingback" tells a blogger you have placed a link to their article in your post. A "Trackback" notifies a blogger you have commented on their material in your post. (Note: Some bloggers turn off the "Trackback" function in WordPress due to concerns about spam.)

Manage Blog Comments

Encouraging comments can be a good start in developing your community. Be prepared, though, to follow up on comments. Have a plan to deal with inappropriate comments and to respond to appropriate ones.

Consider the best way to manage the process and then set up your Discussion Settings. Post a Comment Policy on your blog that notifies visitors of the types of comments that will be allowed and those that will be deleted. Set an example by modeling the tone you want in your blog's discussion areas.

If you or your writing are attacked, you have several options. If a comment is truly inappropriate, you can delete it per your comment policy. Other choices:

- Ignore it. A little controversy may not be totally bad.
- Edit it and explain what you did and why.
- Gently correct it. Respectfully present facts.
- Get someone else to present a countering view.
- Ask for other opinions.

Site Tools and Analysis

Analyzing Traffic

Decide which metrics are important to you in evaluating your website's performance. Keep it simple and then review these metrics regularly.

General Metrics

Your web host probably provides some tools that will help you analyze your traffic. For instance, you may be able to see the Number of Visitors, Unique Visitors (unique IP addresses), Pages Views, and Hits (files requested, note that each image counts as a "hit") for a specific period. The analysis may also show visits by specific Page, Operating System, Browser, Host, Country, Day, Hour, and Duration, as well as by Search Keyphrases and Keywords. You may be able to see Connections made by using your URL directly, through search engines and through external links.

Google Webmaster Tools (www.google.com/webmasters) provides information and resources to help you understand and improve your site. For instance, it will provide a quick overview of your site's health and search traffic. It will notify you of crawl errors and malware and verify the number of pages indexed via sitemaps associated with your site. It will identify top search queries and pages, as well as links to your site.

To use this resource, sign into Google Webmaster Tools with a Google account. Click on "Add a site" and enter your URL. This will take you to a Site verification page that confirms that you own the site.

If you want to conduct more indepth analysis, Google Analytics provides additional tools.

Advertising and Affiliate Networks

If you use Adsense to place ads or have placed ads through an Affiliate Network, those sites will provide additional revenue-related information.

For instance, besides Page Views, Adsense will show you the number of Clicks on ads, the CTC (Click Through %), and RPM (Estimated Revenue per Thousand Impressions).

Affiliate networks will provide reports that show statistics such as Impressions, Clicks, Earnings Per Click and Conversion %.

Subscriptions and Links

If your goal is to build traffic from repeat visitors, you'll be interested in subscription data.

If you use a third party, such as Vertical Response or Aweber, to manage your email lists, they will be able to provide good information on email list subscriptions and readership.

If you use a WordPress plugin, such as Jet Pack, to notify subscribers of new posts, you will see your subscribers under "Users" on the WordPress Dashboard.

If you have set up FeedBurner (feedburner.google.com) you'll be able to track Subscribers to your RSS feed, the reader applications with which they have accessed your blog, Item Views and more.

You can see who is linking to your site with Google Webmaster Tools.

Making Money With Your Website

Your website can help you make money either indirectly or directly.

Indirectly, it can help you make money by increasing your credibility, reach and influence. Your website is an important piece of your personal, organizational or company brand. Your website will help make it easy for people to find you and learn about what you have to offer. It can provide a place to begin to build a community and spread ideas.

Depending on your website purpose, it may also provide opportunities to make money directly. The three major ways to make money with a website are through:
1) **Advertising**
2) **Affiliate Marketing** and
3) **Product Sales**

Advertising

One way of making money from your website or blog is by placing ads on it.

The most common way of doing this is through advertising networks that pay you a few cents when visitors click on an ad ("pay per click") on your site. The most well-known network is Google Adsense. You can apply for an Adsense account through your Google account. Some alternatives to Adsense are:
- Chitika
- Bidvertiser
- Blogads

If you apply to Adsense, increase your chances of acceptance by completing your site and content beforehand. Eliminate empty pages, check links, label images and make sure navigation is working properly. (I got turned down several times on my first site, but kept making improvements until my site was accepted.)

Once accepted, you can select from different sizes and types of advertising blocks and paste code onto your site. Then Adsense places specific ads there that seem to fit with your content and the visitor's interests. If you wish, you can block ads from general categories, specific sensitive categories, specific ad networks or advertiser URLs.

Be sure to familiarize yourself with and follow Adsense's policies. For instance, they have a strict policy prohibiting clicking on your own ads!

These days, it's rather difficult to make a lot of money doing this, as most internet users simply ignore ads on websites, but it's one of several methods that can be combined to monetize your site.

Affiliate Marketing

Another way of making money from a website is through affiliate marketing. As a "publisher" with a website, you can become part of an advertiser's affiliate network. When you place the advertiser's ads on your website, you insert a code that identifies you if someone clicks on the ad. If they then make a purchase, the advertiser pays you a commission.

One way to get started with affiliate marketing is to join networks that connect publishers and advertisers. Examples of these are Commission Junction, ClickBank, Linkshare, ShareASale and Amazon Associates.

As a publisher, you look through networks' lists of advertisers for ones that fit well with your content. Ideally, you find products that a visitor to your site would be likely to buy. You then apply to become an affiliate. Once approved, you paste ads with your personalized code onto your website.

If you'd like to try out affiliate marketing, I recommend starting with Rakuten Linkshare Network. They have a large network of advertisers and make the process easy.

Commission Junction also has a large number of advertisers. Beware, though, because they begin to charge a $10/month "dormant fee" if you go for six months without generating commissions.

ClickBank, mainly known for "knowledge products", such as training courses, typically provides generous commissions. They withhold payments to new affiliates, however, until sales have been accrued using five different credit card numbers and at least two different forms of payment, not including PayPal.

Amazon Associates allows you to earn commissions from products sold from what is now the internet's largest retailer. The program is easy to join and provides a variety of advertising tools, giving associates the opportunity to place banner ads, place product links in reviews, showcase deals and more. This is also an easy way to get started with affiliate marketing, however in recent years Amazon has discontinued the program in certain states.

Another way to participate in affiliate marketing is to approach "good fit" advertisers directly. Look for affiliate programs on their sites and/or ask them if they're interested in a partnership.

Affiliate Marketing Tips:
- Choose reputable, high quality affiliates and affiliate networks. Associate yourself with organizations that will deliver value to customers and payments to you.
- Choose products that fit well with your site content. (Note: Product research and reviews can be helpful to your site visitors. Be sure to adhere to FTC rules related to product promotion, though. Relationships must be disclosed when providing endorsements. Results advertised must be "typical".)
- In choosing products to promote, balance focus and choice. Concentrate marketing on a few relevant quality products and also provide some diversity.

- Read affiliate agreement carefully. For example, what are the requirements, limitations, commission amounts, minimums, payment timing and processes? Be alert to "red flags", such as exclusive agreements, dormant account fees, affiliate charges, and pyramid schemes.
- Don't become frustrated if you are turned down by advertisers, especially in the beginning. If you don't yet have much website traffic, you may not meet their criteria. Sometimes they turn applicants down for other reasons as well — for instance if your state has certain tax policies or if they feel your content isn't a good fit.

Use the following worksheets to develop and manage your affiliate marketing program. Keep organized with all of your individual affiliate and affiliate network information (username, passwords, ID#s, etc.) in one place. Then match affiliate ads with related content on your web pages. You can do this by creating multiple sidebars so that different pages can carry relevant ads.

Affiliate Networks

Network:
Account #:
Username:
Password:

Potential Advertisers	Accepted	Denied	Terms

Network:
Account #:
Username:
Password:

Potential Advertisers	Accepted	Denied	Terms

Network:
Account #:
Username:
Password:

Potential Advertisers	Accepted	Denied	Terms

Affiliate Information

Product/ Website	Affiliate ID	User ID/ Password	Terms/ Commission	Marketing/ Notes

SideBar Strategy Brainstorm: Potential Advertisers

Note major page topics for which you might create specific advertising sidebars.

Then list potential advertisers to place ads for in each sidebar.

Topic 1:	Topic 2:	Topic 3:

Topic 4:	Topic 5:	Topic 6:

SideBar Advertising Strategy

Set up multiple sidebars so that you can place relevant ads near related content. If your theme isn't already set up to allow multiple sidebars, you can do this with a Plugin, such as Simple Page Sidebars. Copy and paste advertising code into the sidebar using a Text widget.

SideBar Name	Ads

SideBar Assignments

Keep track of the sidebars you have assigned to each page of your website.

Page	SideBar

Selling Products

Many website owners make money on the internet by selling products.

To do this, you'll need to have a means of taking orders and setting up delivery of the product, as well as a means of collecting money. Your "shopping cart" and payment processing systems need to work together.

If you plan to sell many different products, you can simplify the process by selecting and installing an eCommerce theme and/or subscribing to a shopping cart service. There are also many eCommerce WordPress plugins available to help you sell products on your site, such as woocommerce and MarketPlace.

eCommerce Plugins

The most popular WordPress eCommerce plugin is woocommerce-excelling eCommerce. When you install woocommerce, it creates several pages on your site, for instance a Cart Page, Checkout Page, Pay Page, Thanks Page, My Account Page, and pages to Edit Address, View Order, Change Password, Logout and find a Lost Password. It provides Tax and Shipping Options, Payment Gateways, email autoresponder and coupon options. Woocommerce makes this basic plugin available free and then supplements it with several paid extensions (and some free ones, too).

Shopping Cart Solutions for Digital Product Sales

Web hosts often partner with and promote general use shopping cart services. Here, I'll just mention a couple of specialized ones that are particularly suited to simplifying digital product sales online.

E-junkie allows you to paste "Buy Now" and "Shopping Cart" buttons into your site to sell either tangible or digital items. For digital product sales, the buyer is redirected to the instant download of your product after a successful payment. Their secure link expires after the maximum number of download attempts and hours you designate for the product. The product PDF is stamped with the buyer's name, email address and unique transaction ID to discourage unauthorized sharing. E-junkie provides multiple payment choices, built-in shipping, sales tax and VAT calculators and discount code options. You can also add an autoresponder (ex. a thank you email with instructions) and even create your own affiliate program. E-junkie charges $5/month. (Note: This would be in addition to your PayPal fees.)

For digital product sales, gumroad is an interesting new option. Gumroad allows you to sell and accept all major credit cards (but not PayPal) for your digital products, such as ebooks, music, comics, software, or film, on your site or through a link. You upload your product to Gumroad and they handle the secure delivery of it. Their total fee is 5% plus a $.25 transaction fee.

Payments

Whether you use a plugin to create your sales process or a shopping cart solution, you'll need a way to accept payments. The easiest way to get started is to take payments via Paypal.

With a PayPal Payments Standard account, you can accept credit card and PayPal payments on your website with a link to PayPal. There is no monthly fee, just a $.30 per transaction fee plus 2.9% of the sale. (For international sales, the rate is 3.9%, plus a fixed fee based on currency received. PayPal does discount their rates for eligible nonprofits and high volume accounts.). Under this plan, you follow PayPal's directions to add a button to your site with a few lines of code. When your customer clicks Checkout, they go to PayPal, and then return to your site after completing the transaction.

If you want the customer to be able to check out directly on your website, rather than link to PayPal, there is an "Advanced" plan for an additional $5/month (plus the normal fees) that works with many shopping cart platforms and also includes a "Bill me later option". (You get paid right away.)

Note: PayPal also now makes it possible to accept payments in person with their PayPal Here mobile app. You download and launch the app from their site to apply for a free card reader. Then, for a 2.7% flat fee, you can swipe your buyer's card through the card reader to obtain payment.

Testimonials: Permission and FTC Rules

Testimonials can be effective in selling, particularly if you use real names, photos, locations and other specific identifiers. If you use testimonials on your site, be sure you have obtained complete permission from the endorser.

When promoting products online, be sure to follow FTC rules regarding product endorsements. Relationships must be disclosed and advertising results presented must be "typical".

Protect and Maintain Your Site

Protecting Your Site

After all the work you've put into creating it, don't forget to take measures to protect your content and your site.

Back Up Your Site Regularly: Institute a process to back up your site regularly. It's best to have a process that happens automatically, so you don't have to remember to do it. If anything happens to your site, you'll be glad you did.

Check your webhosting plan to see what options they offer. For instance, Bluehost includes regular back-ups in their hosting plans and also offers a service with a few more features for an annual fee of around $12.99. Web hosts may not entirely guarantee their back-ups, though, so you may want to supplement any service they provide with another means and keep a back-up copy in another location. For instance, BlueHost has a tutorial video that shows you how to back up your site yourself so you can keep copies of the files and database in a separate location.

Automatic back-up options also include free plugins, such as WordPress Backup to Dropbox, BackupWordPress, BackWPup, UpdraftPlus Backup or XCloner, paid "plugins", such as VaultPress ($55–165/year), or software, such as SiteVault (starting at a $39 one-time fee for up to five sites).

If you use an automatic means of backing up your site, check it occasionally to be sure it's working properly.

Keep Up-to-Date: Make a practice of updating to the newest version of WordPress, plugins, themes and other software so that new security updates are included. (Be sure to have a back-up before you update, just in case something goes awry.) Delete old WordPress plugins.

Avoid Spam: Install a spam plugin. Akismet, a popular antispam plugin that catches comment spam on blogs, is free for personal blogs and websites and $5/month for commercial sites. Other antispam tools include plugins such as Antispam For All Fields, Invisible Captcha (for visitor comments), and CryptX (to hide email addresses from spiders). If you are getting a lot of spam, consider disallowing comments (you can allow them on specific posts or pages only) or unchecking "trackbacking" in your Discussion Settings.

Choose a Reputable, Secure Host: So far, I've been very happy with BlueHost. With another host I used previously, I did experience repeated hacker attacks.

Choose Strong Passwords: A strong password contains at least seven characters and a mixture of upper and lowercase letters, numbers and symbols. Don't use the same password across accounts. Choose different passwords for your hosting and WordPress logins. Make sure your associated email address has a strong password as well.

Don't Use the Default "admin" as your WordPress Username. Choose something different and more complex. This is a big factor in preventing hackers from taking over your site. Change it when you first install WordPress if possible. If you have to change it later, take care to follow WordPress's directions precisely (or get help) to avoid inadvertently deleting content.

Post a Copyright Notice.

Website Maintenance

When your site is complete, don't forget that it will need a little maintenance from time to time.

Website Visitor Experience

Make sure your visitors are having a good experience on your site. Check menus and links occasionally to be sure they are working correctly. A useful plugin for this is Broken Link Checker.

Check Google Webmaster Tools from time to time to identify potential issues that warrant adjustments. For instance, Webmaster Tools will identify "crawl errors" where pages are not found and alert you if it detects malware. You can also submit and test sitemaps there.

Make sure your site is appearing correctly on different browsers and that it loads fairly quickly.

A tool you can use to check out how fast your site loads is Google's PageSpeed Insights (http://developers.google.com/speed/pagespeed/insights). Enter a URL and it will test how fast the page loads on both desktop devices and mobile devices. Then it will provide a summary of suggestions to increase page loading speed.

For non-tech types, some of the suggestions may be difficult to understand without help. One tweak that would likely be in reach, though, would be to optimize images so they load faster. If your photo or graphics program doesn't give you an option to automatically adjust the size of photos for use on the internet (ex. "Image Quality: Web" or "Optimize for Web"), try a free online tool such as Pixlr or Webresizer. Try to keep file sizes to 100 KB or less, and to 50KB or less if there are multiple photos on the same page.

Another easy adjustment to improve loading speed is to delete any plugins you don't need.

Maintenance

Most software and plugins are updated on occasion to make improvements and fix bugs. It is important to keep these up to date.

Make sure you have a process to back up your site regularly so you don't lose all of your good work through some disastrous event.

Be alert to domain and webhosting renewal dates. Review your plan well ahead of the renewal dates — it may be locked and unavailable for transfer around that time.

Even if you don't produce a blog with regular fresh content, you'll want to update your content from time to time. If you have a blog, you'll need a regular process to manage and respond to comments received.

Finally, don't forget to take steps to clean out your email box every now and then, especially if it has limited capacity.

Website Maintenance Plan

What will be your process for each of these maintenance items? How often do you need to perform it?

	Timing/Frequency	Process
Check for Site Errors & Issues (Google Webmaster Tools)		
Check Loading Speed		
Update WordPress/Software		
Update Plugins		
Back Up Website		
Review/Renew Domain		
Review/Renew Webhosting		
Update Content		
Manage Comments		
Cull Email		
Other		

What's Next?

Your Website: What Now?

Congratulations. You've come a long way.

What's left? What else do you need to further develop your website successfully?

Before I leave you, I'd like to address two last issues important for your ongoing success — Your Website Future and Your Support Network.

Your Website Future

Launching your site is a huge accomplishment. Go ahead and celebrate.

Then, look ahead into the future. As in everything else, the Internet world doesn't hold still or stay the same. Use the worksheet on the next page to help set up a system to evaluate your website, anticipate and adjust to change and continue to grow.

Your Support Network

As we have covered in this book, creating a successful website involves a variety of skills, strategies, tools and tactics. No doubt, you have learned a lot and will continue to learn as you move forward and continue to gain experience with internet tools and strategies.

If you are stuck, frustrated, losing interest, or simply too busy to do everything yourself, there are many ways to get free or reasonably-priced help from others. In the next chapter, "More Help", I'll cover a variety of such resources.

Meantime, use the following worksheet, "Your Support Network" to identify the kinds of help you need to finish your website project and continue to progress. While technical help may be an important part of this, you'll see that a range of types of support can make your journey smoother, faster and more fulfilling.

What's Next?

What's next for you depends on many factors. Some new website owners merely check the task off their list and move on to the next task. Others will celebrate, take a deep breath and then plunge into making the most of the increased traffic and visibility the site produces. Some will even move on to creating new sites they have come up with during the process of creating their first one. It's definitely easier the next time around!

No matter what your current next steps are, you now have a new skill and access to a creative tool that opens up a world of new possibilities.

Thanks for taking this journey with me and best wishes to you for your continued success!

Your Website Future

Look ahead into the future. Set up systems to evaluate your website, anticipate and adjust to change, and continue to progress.

How will you measure your success?

How will you keep your website (and yourself) current?

What changes can you anticipate?

What opportunities can you prepare for?

What's next?

Your Support Network

Creating and maintaining a website is a big accomplishment. For most, it requires learning, patience, discipline, inspiration, ideas, and often practical help as well.

Whose help do you need to be successful? Sometimes your help comes from specific individuals and services they provide, but it can also come from publications, websites, support forums, groups or courses.

In addition to practical advice, it can help to have role models to look to for motivation and trusted friends or colleagues to look to for honest feedback. If you are working mainly on your own, it may be useful to have someone to help you be accountable.

What type of support do you need? Where can you find it?

✓ Vision

✓ Tech Help

✓ Feedback

✓ "Moral Support"

✓ Learning

✓ Discipline

✓ Inspiration

✓ Resources & Tools

✓ Other

More Help

Need More Help?

This books has covered the basics of creating a website, but obviously cannot cover everything you might run into. Fortunately, many additional resources are available when you need additional help.

"Do It Yourself" Resources

As there are many free and inexpensive tools and so much information available on the internet, it is possible these days for you to do it all yourself.

Free Help

Many free resources are available to help you create and build your site. If you are patient, willing to search a little and read through "documentation" or forums of the services you use, a wealth of free information is available online.

"Documentation" is information provided for a computer program that describes its structure, requirements, operation, maintenance, known defects, enhancements, etc.

"Forums" are online discussion sites where people can hold conversations and post messages on specific topics. Developers often use forums to uncover and address common problems and users often give each other tips. If you are having a problem or have a question, it's likely that it's already been addressed for someone else, so searching a forum is often a quick way to find a solution.

Web Host: Along with their customer service and technical help resources, web hosts often provide other resources to guide you through processes and solve problems. For instance, BlueHost has a series of videos that demonstrate the steps to go through to set up your website.

WordPress Help: WordPress is fairly easy, but as with anything else, using it involves a learning curve. Often it takes experimenting a bit to get the hang of it. On WordPress's top right-hand corner, you'll find a drop-down "Help" menu that will guide you to documentation and forums on specific topics.

Themes: Premium themes often come with support and/or forums that can be helpful.

Plugins: Most plugins invite you to "Visit plugin site" for more information and help resources.

Additional Online Resources: Of course, if you do an internet search using a phrase related to your issue, you are likely to find additional forums, YouTube videos or other resources.

Learning Resources

Website Design and WordPress: If you want more personalized help learning WordPress, I recommend resources provided by Angela Willis of Website Design Mojo. She offers a six-week video course, along with weekly Q&A webinars, daily email coaching and more. While this does involve an investment, it is still a lot less expensive than having someone else create your website, and you will own your skills.

Graphics: You can learn to create your own banners, buttons, headers, and ads with Gimp, a free graphics program. Angela Willis also offers an inexpensive self-study video course to get you started, Gimp Graphics Mojo.

Hired Help

While it is possible to undertake all the elements of putting up a website yourself, there are also many relatively inexpensive ways to get help if you need or want it. Here are some resources to consider:

On elance, you can submit a job you would like done to their stable of more than 2 million freelancers. Interested freelancers will respond with proposals, including their credentials. Freelancers may work on a fixed-price basis for the project or at an hourly rate. The fees proposed by the freelancers include a commission to elance. Examples of projects: administrative support, IT support, design, writing, translation, legal, finance, sales and marketing, engineering and manufacturing. Their site provides templates to guide you to include appropriate information in your posting.

oDesk gives you easy access to 3 million freelancers who can be hired for either an hourly or fixed price. Your price includes oDesk's commission. Available services include: web development, business services, customer service, administrative support, design, writing and translation, software development, and IT support. You can browse a list of freelancers with skills needed for your type of project — including location, hourly rate, skills, tests, portfolio, hours and projects worked. You can either post a job so that any freelancers can respond with a proposal or contact individual freelancers directly.

Crowdspring specializes in logos, design and naming. Here, you name the price you want to pay for a project and your deadline. Minimums are given for the type of project, along with a range of rates for different levels of service. Interested designers and writers respond with their designs. You then can choose the one you like best.

99designs also specializes in design projects. Here, you also submit a design brief describing your project, choose from three price levels and launch a design contest. You can then choose your favorite from multiple designs submitted.

If you need a Virtual Assistant on a regular basis, check out VirtualStaffFinder. For a fee, Chris Ducker's company will help you locate and hire qualified workers based in the Philippines to do administrative tasks, web development, content creation or SEO work.

Resources Mentioned

Webhosting and Domains

Overall Recommendations:
- BlueHost: www.bluehost.com
- FatCow: www.fatcow.com
- HostGator: www.hostgator.com (Use coupon code: IFICANYOUCAN for 25% off)

Special Features:
- GoDaddy: www.godaddy.com (bulk domains, domain masking)
- NameCheap: www.namecheap.com (free WHOIS privacy)
- DreamHost: www.dreamhost.com (free for qualifying non-profits or use coupon code DREAMYSITE for $40 off first year hosting)

Software

- www.WordPress.org (for sites that will be hosted elsewhere) WordPress software also may be downloaded directly via web hosts.
- www.WordPress.com (for sites that will be hosted free via WordPress) (Note: these cannot be commercial sites.)
- WordPress support: www.wordpress.org/support
- Weebly: for very simple sites, available through BlueHost, FatCow or HostGator

WordPress Themes and Templates

- ThemeForest: www.themeforest.net
- ElegantThemes: www.elegantthemes.com
- StudioPress (Genesis framework): www.studiopress.com
- diyThemes (Thesis): www.diythemes.com
- Artisteer: www.artisteer.com

Photos

Free:
- www.freedigitalphotos.net
- www.morguefile.com
- www.wpclipart.com
- www.stockfreeimages.com
- www.sxc.hu
- www.wikimedia.org

Low-cost:
- www.dreamstime.com
- www.istockphoto.com

Keyword Research
- Google Keyword Planner (requires an Adwords account): www.google.com/adwords
- Übersuggest: www.ubersuggest.org
- SEMrush: www.semrush.com
- SEO Book: www.seobook.com

SEO Plugins
- All in One SEO pack: www.semperplugins.com
- SEO Plugin by Yoast: www.yoast.com

Site Analysis
- Google Webmaster Tools: www.google.com/webmasters/tools
- Google Analytics: www.google.com/analytics

Graphics tools
- Gimp: www.gimp.org
- Pixlr: www.pixlr.com
- Webresizer: www.webresizer.com

Blog Directories & Feeds
- Technorati www.technorati.com
- Blogcatalog: www.blogcatalog.com
- Feedburner: www.feedburner.com

List Management/Marketing
- aWeber: www.aweber.com
- Vertical Response: www.verticalresponse.com
- Constant Contact: www.constantcontact.com
- MailChimp: www.mailchimp.com

Advertising Networks
- Google Adsense: www.google.com/adsense
- Bidvertiser: www.bidvertiser.com
- Chitika: www.chitika.com
- Blogads: www.blogads.com

Affiliate Marketing
- LinkShare/Rakmuten: www.linkshare.com
- ShareASale: www.shareasale.com
- Amazon Associates: https://affiliate-program.amazon.com
- Commission Junction: www.cj.com

Shopping Carts/Payments
- Paypal: www.paypal.com
- E-junkie: www.e-junkie.com
- Gumroad: www.gumroad.com

Design/Miscellaneous Freelance Help
- elance: www.elance.com
- oDesk: www.odesk.com
- crowdspring: www.crowdspring.com
- 99designs: www.99designs.com
- VirtualStaffFinder: www.virtualstafffinder.com

Website Design and Graphics
- Website Design Mojo (WordPress Training): www.marketersmojo.com
- Graphics Mojo Coaching (Learn Gimp): www.marketersmojo.com

Social Media
- Hootsuite: www.hootsuite.com
- Onlywire: www.onlywire.com

Other Useful Tools
Internet Research
- www.whois.com/whois: Domain registration information
- www.domainsigma.com: Website analysis and WHOIS reports
- www.alexa.com: Demographics, traffic and usage statistics for specific websites.
- www.browsershots.org: Check to see how website screenshots appear on different browsers. (Suggested: Firefox, Internet Explorer, Chrome, Safari, Opera)
- www.surveymonkey.com: Conduct your own surveys.

Definitions

Affiliate Marketing: A marketing arrangement whereby a party with marketing resources, such as a website, blog, mailing list or salesforce, undertakes marketing activities to sell another business' product in exchange for a commission when a sale is made.

Archive: Past blog posts. Often organized by date, but also can be organized by category, by author, or alphabetically.

Autoresponder: A program that automatically sends a prepared response or series of responses to emails or orders received.

Blog: A "weblog" or online journal. A blog typically displays entries in reverse chronological order (most recent first).

Blogroll: A list of links to other blogs.

Browser: A software application used to navigate the internet that makes it possible to locate, retrieve and display content. (Ex. Google Chrome, Firefox, Internet Explorer)

Categories: On a blog, a list of broad topics to help organize related posts and make it possible for readers to find content.

Content Management System (CMS): A computer program used to create, manage, store and deploy content on Web pages. WordPress is a CMS that uses the PHP platform.

cPanel: A popular Unix-based webhosting control panel used for website management.

CSS: Cascading Style Sheet. These are used to create a consistent website page layout and appearance by defining style elements such as fonts, color, and formatting.

Domain: An internet address, beginning with "www.", followed by a website name, and ending with a "top-level domain", such as ".com" or ".org".

Feeds: Feeds allow users to keep up with the latest news and information from other sites. Feedreaders automatically look for new content and provide updates.

Footer: The area at the bottom of a website that stays constant.

FTP: File Transfer Protocol, needed to transfer files from one host to another over the internet.

Header: The area at the top of a website that stays constant. It typically includes a logo and a navigation menu.

HTML: HyperText Markup Language. The primary type of computer programming code for creating web pages and information displayed in a web browser.

ICANN: International Corporation of Assigned Names and Numbers. A nonprofit organization responsible for coordinating the global internet's systems of unique identifiers.

Keywords: Words or phrases that describe content. The words that would be typed into the search box when conducting a web search.

Link: A word, group of words, URL or image you can click on to go to a new page or new section.

Open Source Software (OSS): Free computer software available to anyone for any purpose. Users have the freedom to run, copy, distribute, study, change and improve the software. WordPress is an open source project.

Opt-in: Agree to participate. Per the FTC's requirements, to send mass emails legally, you must first get intended recipients to "opt-in" to your list.

Permalinks: Permanent URLs for individual blog posts. WordPress provides a choice of permalink structures, so you can choose one that is both reader and SEO-friendly.

PHP: A programming language used by WordPress.

Pingback: Tells a blogger that you have placed a link to their article in your post.

Plugin: A software extension that adds a feature to an existing software program.

Posts: Individual entries in a blog.

Public Domain: In regard to copyrights, works in the "public domain" are available for use without any copyright fees or additional permissions.

Responsive: In regard to websites, the design allows it to adjust for optimal viewing on different types of screens.

Royalty-free: Copyrighted material that, after an initial fee has been paid, doesn't require additional payment of fees every time it is used.

RSS feed: "Rich Site Summary" or Really Simple Syndication". Feed that automatically updates information for subscribers.

Sidebar: A column on either the right or left side of a web page.

SEO: Search Engine Optimization. The process of increasing visibility of a website in unpaid search engine results.

Shortlink: A shortened URL.

Sitemap: A list of pages of a website.

Tags: On a blog, labels that identify specific topics and make it possible for readers to find content.

Theme: The basic design across the pages of your site, typically defining elements such as color, fonts and layout, and sometimes adding functionality through pre-formatted templates.

Trackback: Notifies a blogger that you have commented on their material in your post.

Unlimited Sites: Feature advertised by web hosts that allows hosting of multiple domains on one hosting account at no extra charge. (Note: Additional fees are still required for additional domain registration.)

Unsubscribe: In email marketing, the FTC requires email senders to include an option for the recipient to unsubscribe from their list.

Webhosting: The service that stores and makes a website accessible via the internet.

Widget: A small application that adds a function or content to a web page.

URL: Uniform Resource Locator. Location of a page on the internet.

About the Author

Jane Moyer is a communication specialist and talent developer.

She has been fascinated by the idea of regular people being able to create and disseminate their own content since she stumbled upon a cable company public access television studio while a student at Michigan State University back in the last century. After earning a master's degree from the College of Communication Arts & Sciences there, Jane had a long and exciting career working for Home Box Office in affiliate sales, marketing and management. She held every job from Regional Coordinator to Senior Vice President. Since then, as a business and career coach, she has worked with a diverse range of smart forward-thinking leaders at all levels to upgrade skills and update strategies to thrive in this era of change, challenge and opportunity.

Today's tech and communication tools now make it possible for anyone to create their own books, videos and websites and for ideas to spread quickly around the globe. In this book, Jane combines her love for creative expression with her background in communication, marketing, talent development and business to show regular, non-technical folks without big budgets how to get their message out into the world by creating their own website or blog.

31099063R00084

Made in the USA
Charleston, SC
08 July 2014